CARDBOARD FURNITURE

STEP-BY-STEP TECHNIQUES AND DESIGNS

Other Schiffer Books on Related Subjects:

Naturally Furnished: Rustic Designs by Women Artisans,
978-0-7643-3325-5, $16.99

How-to with Bamboo: Simple Instructions and Projects,
0-7643-2416-0, $14.95

A Beginner's Guide to Mosaics: Four Decorative Projects,
978-0-7643-4096-3, $19.99

I dedicate this work to Theo.

Thank you to the team that allowed me to make my project a reality and guided me through to the culmination of the work.

To the photographers, Miguel Duvivier and Franck Schmitt.

To Eric Guiomar, who introduced me to the intersecting crosspiece technique, for his warm welcome and great ideas…

To Blandine, Madame Cardboard, for her recipe for imitation cement on cardboard.

To Faustine, Veronica, Jocelyne, Karine, Marie, and Miguel for being there.

To Anne and Pascal for putting their trust in me and for sharing the workshop.

To Laurencia and Gilles, Isabelle and Pascal, for welcoming me in their homes so I could present my work there.

Thank you to all my clients and the numerous trainees for putting their trust in me and for sharing your ideas and creations.

And to all those who participated in this ecological approach by supplying me with cardboard, and who supported me along the way. I will not name them all here because there are just too many and I wouldn't want to forget anyone. They will know who they are…THANK YOU to everyone for allowing me to practice an activity that I am passionate about.

Workshops, courses, custom designs…
Find up-to-date information for KIKI CARTON at
www.kikicarton.com

Design Director : Laurent Quellet
Graphic Design: Isabelle Mayer
Layout : Christine Loiseau

Originally published as *Le Grande Livre des Meubles en Carton: Techniques et créations en pas à pas* by Fleurus Éditions.

Translated from French by Phoebe Green for Omicron Language Solutions, LLC.

Cover by Justin Watkinson
Type set in Impact/Formata/Scala Sans

ISBN: 978-0-7643-4151-9
Printed in China

Published by Schiffer Publishing, Ltd.
4880 Lower Valley Road
Atglen, PA 19310
Phone: (610) 593-1777; Fax: (610) 593-2002
E-mail: Info@schifferbooks.com

For the largest selection of fine reference books on this and related subjects, please visit our website at
www.schifferbooks.com.
You may also write for a free catalog.

This book may be purchased from the publisher.
Please try your bookstore first.

We are always looking for people to write books on new and related subjects. If you have an idea for a book, please contact us at:
proposals@schifferbooks.com.

Schiffer Books are available at special discounts for bulk purchases for sales promotions or premiums. Special editions, including personalized covers, corporate imprints, and excerpts can be created in large quantities for special needs. For more information contact the publisher.

In Europe, Schiffer books are distributed by
Bushwood Books
6 Marksbury Ave.
Kew Gardens
Surrey TW9 4JF England
Phone: 44 (0) 20 8392 8585; Fax: 44 (0) 20 8392 9876
E-mail: info@bushwoodbooks.co.uk
Website: www.bushwoodbooks.co.uk

THE GREAT BOOK OF
CARDBOARD FURNITURE
Step-by-Step Techniques and Designs

KIKI CARTON

Photographs by
Miguel Duvivier and Franck Schmitt

Schiffer Publishing Ltd

4880 Lower Valley Road • Atglen, PA 19310

CONTENTS

PREFACE

Design has been a passion of mine since childhood. I therefore naturally headed towards hands-on crafts that involved working with volumes, colors, and diverse materials.

To start, display training led me to event planning, exhibitions, and trade shows for some years. I then acquired some training as a model maker dedicated to special events, furnishing, and decoration, interning with two master teachers from whom I learned a great deal. I was then responsible for design, production, and project management of trade shows in Paris and the Grand-Ouest region of France. This led to 18 years of experience working closely with designers, decorators, carpenters, and display designers. The world of trade show design is in perpetual motion, so knowing how to work in a short amount of time is key.

On Easter 2004, I had a transformative meeting with Eric Guiomar, creator of a technique (honeycomb and cross-pieces) for constructing cardboard furniture, which led to training in Paris.

Enthralled by colors and shapes, curious about working with raw materials, particularly now in cardboard, I devoted myself completely to the art of designing furniture and other decorative objects in cardboard, from the ground up.

My model-making job allowed me to work with cardboard in designing for my clients. The idea of creating furniture and accessories out of recycled cardboard seemed logical to me, and important at a worrying time for our environment and the fate of our planet. Tons of cardboard are thrown away every year.

In line with this approach, I generally use handmade Nepalese paper to cover my furniture: it is ecologically sound and comes from a shrub known as lokta which grows back every six to eight years. Moreover, I paint and varnish with water-based or eco-friendly substances. I do not use harmful products.

I mainly work for individuals who want to acquire a unique piece; I create for them and their design aesthetic. But I also work for environmentally aware businesses and for theater productions, designing light, easily-transportable sets from recycled material. In my workshops, I introduce cardboard construction to those who wish to create their own pieces and who enjoy spending pleasant moments together in the studio. I also visit schools to show students these techniques with which they can create their own environments. Cardboard is a material that means a lot to young people.

This is why for six years I have been "cardboarding"…there is no limit to this craft; all shapes and styles are allowed. My studio is my universe, my second home where all are welcome to discover the many aspects of this activity and free to explore their imaginations.

KIKI CARTON

NOTE: Metric has been used for all dimensions, followed by a rounded conversion in inches.

INTRODUCTION

Cardboard

The cardboard used for furniture comes from salvaged material (packaging from bicycles, windscreens, household appliances, lawnmowers, beds, etc.). These large boxes allow an entire furniture panel to be cut from a single sheet. Often thrown away by the ton, this cardboard is just waiting to be used. Salvaging it is thus a creative and useful method of recycling: giving the cardboard a new life. Choose the cardboard according to the size of the furniture you plan to make.

The most useful type is double-wall, corrugated cardboard. Single wall will be more useful for covering smaller or hard to reach parts. Being less solid, it will not be used for the actual construction of furniture. Depending on the furniture in question, you can double-line the outside and/or the base, or use tri-wall cardboard. For the outside of the furniture, choose a piece of cardboard that doesn't have any visible creases, marks, or holes. You can, however, use flawed cardboard for inner sections.

The direction of the cardboard is important for the strength of the piece of furniture—corrugation flutes should run perpendicular to the ground—that is to say, vertically. Intersecting crosspieces will increase solidity.

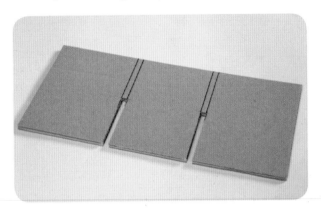

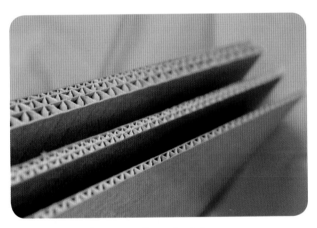

From top to bottom: fluted triple, double, and single.

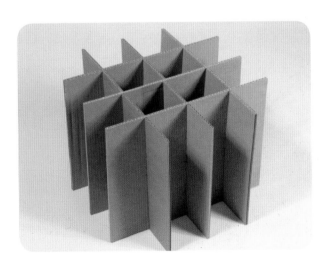

Joining Sheets of Cardboard

When you are covering the surface of a piece of furniture for which the cardboard isn't large enough, it is possible to make a joint between two sheets of equal thickness by gluing them at their edges. Nevertheless, even if you choose two sheets that are both double-wall for example, one may be thicker than the other, making the joint more rather than less visible. Similarly, a connection would be more discreet on the inside of a curve than the outside. To finish, don't forget to cover each joint with kraft tape.

For larger designs, it is difficult to find a sheet that will cover the whole front face of the piece of furniture. In this instance, you can make a joint as you would for the sides. The joint must be very carefully done in order to be as invisible as possible.

To find the stronger side of a sheet of cardboard, look at the corrugation flutes on the cut edge; the thinner flutes are usually on the stronger side (also the side on which printing appears). This is the side that should go on the outside of the piece of furniture.

Tools

For Cutting Out

Utility Knife (box cutter): With a retractable snap-off blade (18 mm [3/4"]) that can be set to avoid cutting oneself or breaking long blades. Blades wear out very quickly; change them regularly in order to achieve the cleanest cut possible.

Jigsaw: A simple model will do, with a fine-toothed blade (for metal or Plexiglas) that will allow you to cut several sheets at once. The shoe of the saw should always be as flat as possible against the cardboard.

Cutting Rule (80 cm [32"]): The same type used in framing.

Cutting Mat (60 x 90 cm [24 x 35"]): large enough to cut out everything without damaging the worktable.

Scissors: For cutting the kraft tape used in drawers or on the inside of the cases, and for cutting the paper that will cover each design.

For Gluing and Assembling

Electric Glue Gun: Hot glue allows quick-drying assembly of cardboard sheets. Be careful of burns, because the nozzle becomes very hot. Do not remove the rubber protection piece during the gluing process. It is better to buy glue sticks (1.5 cm [5/8"] in diameter) in quantity because they are cheaper.

All-Purpose Wallpaper Paste: This glue in powder form is dissolved in water to glue all sorts of paper coverings: tissue paper, newspaper, kraft paper, Nepalese paper, fiber, decorative paper, etc.

White Glue: From a can or bottle, for gluing paper thicker than those mentioned above or specialty papers, like Skivertex.

For Measuring and Drawing

Flexible Tape Measure (like that of a dressmaker): or a metal one for measuring curves.

50 cm (20") Metal Ruler: Very convenient for measuring the insides of the cases. Choose a ruler graded with zero at the edge of the ruler. One meter rulers are also available.

Carpenter's Try Square: preferably long and metal, to cut cardboard sheets at right angles. Position the heel against the thickness of the cardboard, not on top of it, in order to draw a straight right-angled line.

For Finishing

Sandpaper: In different grades (coarse, medium, and fine: 50, 80 and 120) to attach to a sanding block. Sanding can blend joints and edges before covering with kraft tape to hide corrugations.

A Foam Sanding Block: To which you will attach the sheets of sandpaper. If you don't have a sanding block, you can staple the sandpaper to a simple block of wood.

A Wood Rasp: For smoothing areas that are difficult to reach.

A Roll of Kraft Tape: The average width is 3.5 cm (1 3/8"), but you can use wider or narrower tape depending on the area that needs covering.

A Sponge: To moisten the kraft tape. Wet it first and place it in a small container.

Tissue Paper, Newspaper, or Kraft Paper: To prepare surfaces for painting, in order to achieve a more even finish.

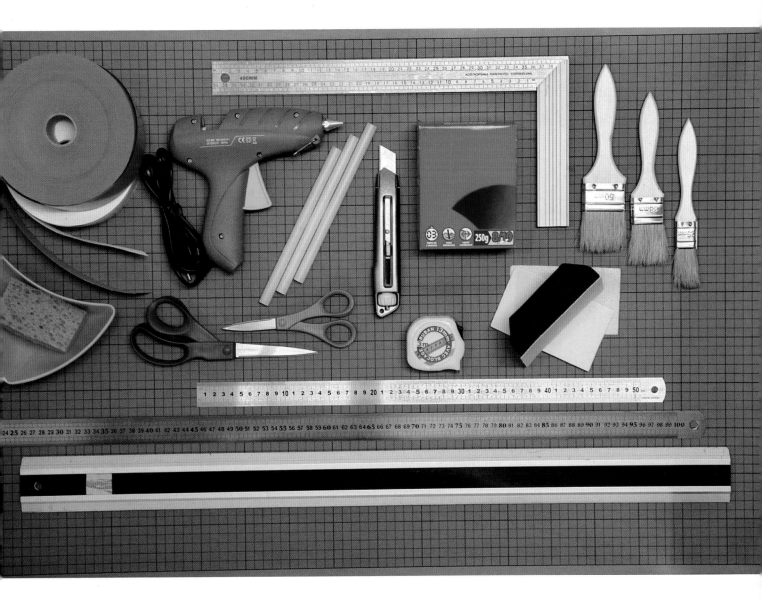

Decorative Paper or Acrylic Paint for Decoration:
There are lines of "organic" paint made with either linseed or sunflower oil. They are a little more expensive, but are of good quality and odorless. I generally use Nepalese paper, plain or patterned, or fiber paper (coconut, mulberry, or banana), to cover furniture. Nepalese paper comes in sheets 50 cm x 70 cm (20 x 28"), but the dimensions can vary slightly because they are handmade and their edges are not always straight. In craft or stationery stores, you will find all sorts of paper to use. It is important to do a preliminary test by applying it to cardboard to see how it reacts to drying and varnishing.

Drawer Pulls: Screws may be included. Otherwise, get matching screws, as well as metal washers, to put between the cardboard and the nut on the back of the drawer.

Colorless Parquet Sealant or Varnish (matte or satin finish)**:** Avoid a gloss finish as it highlights the smallest flaws. Choose water-based or natural types; solvent free and odorless products dry quickly to waterproof and protect your furniture. Three fine coats are needed, but make sure that you allow each coat to dry before applying the next.

Miscellaneous

Drawing pencil, eraser, black marker, brushes for painting and for wallpaper paste, and a tube for rolling cardboard sheets to give them the necessary curvature.

It is also possible to bend the sheets over the edge of a table. You will also need a drill or a borer to attach handles to drawers.

General Construction Principles

Furniture with Cases and a Back

1. Depending on the desired piece of furniture, be sure to have enough sheets of cardboard at your disposal. The number of sheets (listed in the materials section for each design) will vary according to the depth of the design. Also allow for an additional 2 or 3 cm (3/4 or 1 1/8") around the lines to be cut (top and sides) to make cutting through layers with the jigsaw easier. These extra measurements will make following the curves much easier, without having to work right up to the edge of the cardboard. Finally, you will need extra double-wall cardboard for the crosspieces and to line the cases, as well as for the outer covering of the furniture. The sheets intended for the outside of the piece must not have any tears, holes, or staples.

2. Trim the base of each cardboard sheet with the utility knife to leave a clean, flat edge (which will be the bottom of the piece of furniture), positioning the corrugations vertically and using the try square. Lay the sheets of cardboard on top of each other, making sure their bases are aligned, and fasten them together by applying kraft tape along the outside.

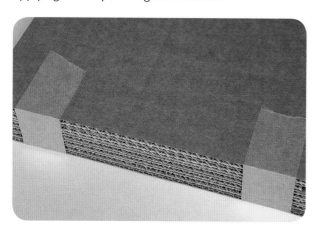

3. Following the pattern measurements, draw the general shape of the piece in pencil, then go over these lines again using a black marker pen, making your lines permanent.

4. Cut along the outside lines of the piece using the jigsaw, making sure you cut through all the layers. Refasten with kraft tape as you cut so the sheets do not slip. Lightly sand down the cut areas.

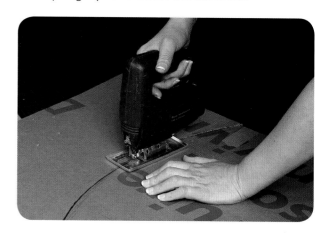

Tips for using the jigsaw
If you are using a jigsaw for the first time, do a test-run by cutting several sheets of cardboard that have been fixed together in a straight line or along a curve. Position the foot of your jigsaw flat against the surface to avoid a slanted cut. When there are many layers together, you can cut into the first sheet with the utility knife, thus guiding the saw.

5. Remove the bottom sheet, cutting the kraft tape away. Then number the sheets from 1 to X with 1 being the front, working backwards in order. Reattach the sheets together (except the back one) and cut out the cases with the jigsaw, making sure you cut through all the layers.

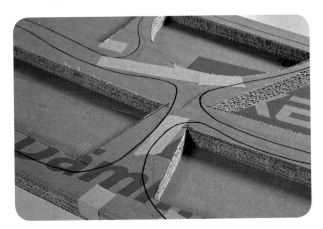

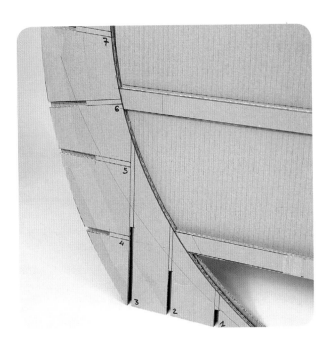

6. On sheet 2, draw the slots shown on the pattern for each piece of furniture (but do not draw on the top or bottom sheets), marking out the middle. They are usually 0.7 cm (0.275") in width, which corresponds to the thickness of double wall cardboard. If your panels have a curve, the edge of your lines will be slanted. In that case, go from the shorter side to calculate the middle of the slot.

8. Following the pattern provided for each of the pieces, mark all of the crosspieces on double-wall cardboard—including their slots—which will be inserted into the central panels, and cut them out one-by-one with the utility knife. They are all the same length, which corresponds to the depth of the furniture, but their height will vary depending on their position.

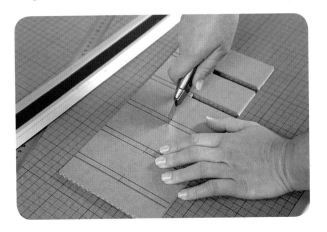

7. With a utility knife, cut the slots of the central sheets that are fastened together (that is to say, from sheet number 2 to the sheet one from the back), only cutting half-way across (solid black lines will be provided on the design for each piece of furniture). Number the slots, making the structure easier to assemble. Then put sheet number 2 against the bottom sheet to draw on where the cuts for the slots are; repeat for the slots on the back of sheet number 1. Marking where the slots are on both sheet number 1 and the back sheet (although we do not cut these) will serve as reference points when assembling the crosspieces.

Tips for positioning crosspieces
The crosspieces at the center of a piece of furniture should have their corrugation flutes as vertical as possible because weight is carried on these vertical corrugations. On the outside of the piece, the direction is less important.

9. Fit all of the crosspieces into the slots on the central panels to form the skeleton of the furniture.

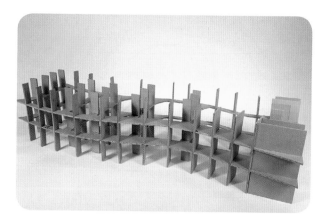

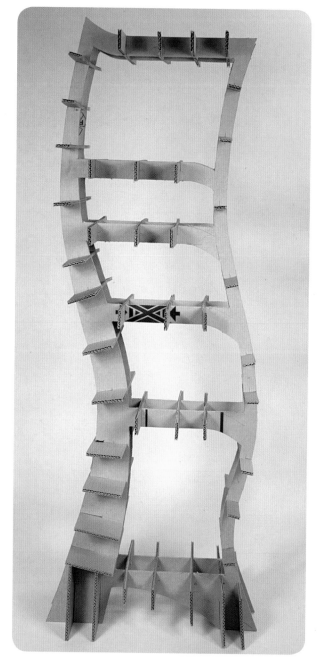

10. Place the back sheet (sheet X) on a work table and lay the whole structure down, with the crosspieces against the lines traced in step 7. Use the glue gun to place a bead of glue on the surface of each crosspiece to fix them to the back. Once the crosspieces are glued to the back, repeat the procedure on the front sheet (sheet 1) of the design.

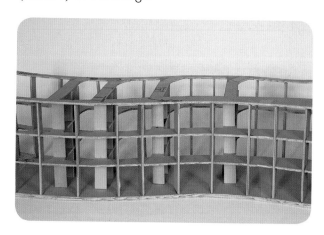

Tips for putting crosspieces together
When the "skeleton" (or structure) has been assembled, do not glue the intersections. Allow for movement where center panels and crosspieces fit together.

11. Line the inside of the cases, at the top and the bottom, with double-wall cardboard. To do this, measure the width, then the depth from the base to the front covering. The visible corrugations on the edges of the cardboard must be positioned towards the front and bottom. Cut the sheets with the utility knife. Fasten them with a thin line of glue from the glue gun on the back edge of the sheet. Once dry, glue the front edge of the sheet with a thin line of glue behind the rim of the front panel. Still using double-wall cardboard, now cut the sheets for the sides of the cases. If the sides are curved, measure the height with a tape measure. Allow for a little more height, say 1 to 2 mm (1/32 to 1/16"), and mold the sheets over the edge of a table or with a tube to give them a curved shape which will follow the furniture's design. Do a test fitting without glue, then apply when ready.

12. Cover each exterior side of the furniture with one (or several) strips of double wall cardboard of the same width as the depth of the furniture, positioning the corrugations to face out, so the cardboard bends more easily. This way the cardboard bends following its interior corrugations, which is not the case otherwise. Mold the sheets for the rounded sections, as below. To cover the whole piece, you will more than likely have to join several sheets together (see "Joining Sheets of Cardboard," p. 8). Be sure to square the bottom of the sheet. Using the glue gun, glue the inner edges of the cut sheets, proceeding in approximately 20 cm (8") sections, as the glue will set very quickly.

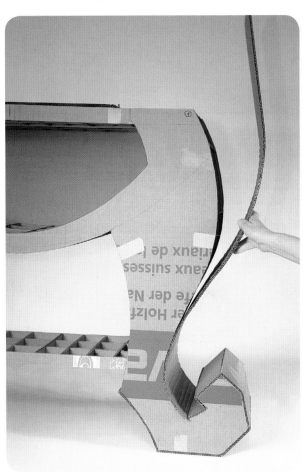

Tips for covering the exterior
Start by covering the underside, or the feet, of the design and continue up the sides, finishing at the top. Do not cover the whole unit with a single sheet of cardboard because each edge must be sharp, not rounded.

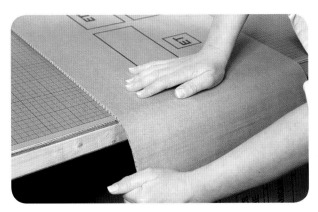

13. Sand down the whole outside surface of the furniture. When sanding along the visible corrugations and ridges of the furniture, keep your block flat in order not to damage the edges.

14. Remove the dust from the sanding process. Stick kraft tape along all visible corrugations, as well as along the inside and outside edges of the cases.
On curves, place kraft tape along the cut edge, notching with scissors before folding and sticking down.

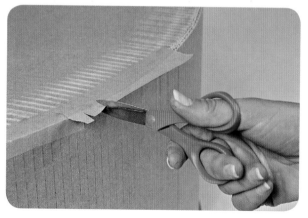

Tips for applying kraft tape

To apply a long strip of kraft tape, tear the strip into shorter pieces and overlap them. Tearing the kraft tape, rather than cutting it, keeps the overlap from becoming too thick. To position strips of kraft tape on the inside edges of cases or drawers, you can fold the strip in two for an easier fit. In this case, the cut of the kraft tape should have clean edges, therefore cut it with scissors. If you don't know how to position kraft tape, don't forget that it is used to conceal visible corrugations on the design. If you are applying the tape along a straight line, this will not cause a problem, but if you are trying to stick it along a curve or corner, you will have to notch it in order to fold it over, much as in sewing.

15. If you wish to paint your furniture, first cover the entire piece with tissue paper, newspaper, or kraft paper. Paper should be torn, rather than cut with scissors, so that the edges of the paper do not show under the paint. Glue the paper on with wallpaper paste, covering the whole item and overlapping each piece of paper slightly so no cardboard is visible. This procedure is necessary to prepare the surface for painting. Leave it to dry so that water in the glue can evaporate completely from the cardboard. Even if it seems dry to the touch, the underside will still be moist…so leave it to dry for 24 hours.

16. Paint your furniture with water-based paint (satin or matte-finish acrylic), applying two or three coats and letting each dry before applying the next. Paint that only requires one coat is also available. If you want to cover your furniture with Nepalese or decorative paper, you can glue it on directly with wallpaper paste. If your Nepalese paper is patterned, you have to remember that this is a handmade paper, so aligning the pattern is not always easy—sometimes even impossible. As for unpatterned Nepalese paper, there is a different color on each side. You can therefore play with the colors, creating a patchwork of torn paper which will add substance and texture.

If you choose to cover your furniture with fiber paper or some other translucent material, depending on the color you want for the finished product, you will probably need a coat of white paint first. Doing this will highlight the fibers or the inherent color patterns without changing them.

17. Once your surface (paint or paper) is dry enough, apply three coats of colorless varnish, letting each coat dry before applying the next.

Furniture with Drawers

1. Build furniture with cases, into which the drawers will slide, following steps 1-14 above.

2. Following the plan provided, draw and cut out the drawer fronts from double-wall cardboard (or better still, use leftover cut-outs from step 5). Corrugations must be positioned vertically on the front of the drawer. If the sides of the piece curve out, the direction of the corrugations must be horizontal in order to follow the curve. In this case, line the front of the drawers with another sheet of cardboard of the same size (with the corrugations vertical) and attach with the glue gun. You can glue together the two sheets of cardboard before marking the outline of the front so you only need to cut once with the jigsaw. Sand down the edge and apply kraft tape all around it. For this, position the strip over the edge and fold it over each side, notching the kraft tape if the front curves.

If your drawers have identical curves, use a template to outline each front piece.

3. Still using the double-wall cardboard, draw and cut out the bottoms of the drawers, making them 1 cm (3/8") less deep than the cases. As for width, they must be able to slide in and out without sticking.

Then, draw and cut out the two lateral sides of each drawer, following the shape of the furniture. Corrugations must be horizontal if the sides curve. Drawer depth is the same as that of the bottom of the drawer; height must be 1 cm (3/8") shorter than the top of the case to avoid sticking. Depending on what design you are making, you may have to bend the cardboard for the sides.

4. Attach the two side pieces to the bottom of the drawer. Put the bottom of the drawer flat on the work table, and attach the cut edges of the sides to the edges of the bottom with a thin line of hot glue. Pay attention to the direction of the curves, if there are any.

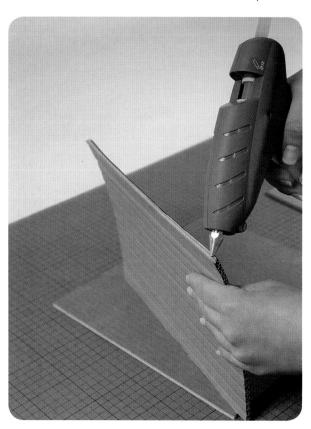

5. Run kraft tape along the inside of the joint on both sides of the drawer.

6. On the back of each front piece, draw a line 7 mm (1/4 - 3/8") from the bottom. Then make a mark in the middle of this line.

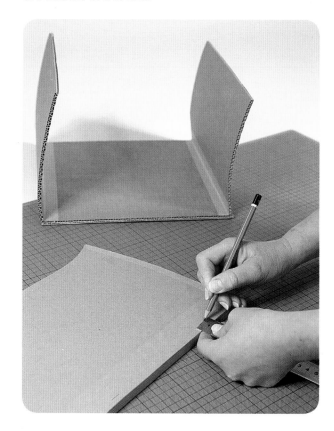

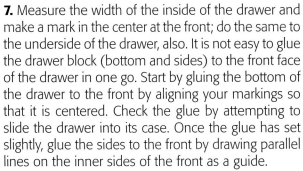

7. Measure the width of the inside of the drawer and make a mark in the center at the front; do the same to the underside of the drawer, also. It is not easy to glue the drawer block (bottom and sides) to the front face of the drawer in one go. Start by gluing the bottom of the drawer to the front by aligning your markings so that it is centered. Check the glue by attempting to slide the drawer into its case. Once the glue has set slightly, glue the sides to the front by drawing parallel lines on the inner sides of the front as a guide.

8. To make the back section, place the drawer on a sheet of double-wall cardboard and draw the inside outline. Then draw a line to connect the tops of the side lines, and cut out the resulting shape with the utility knife.

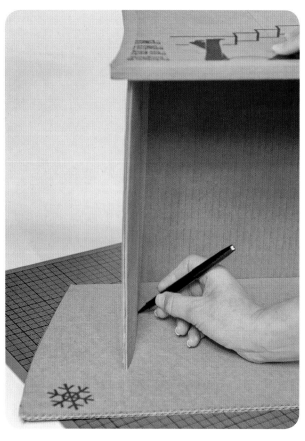

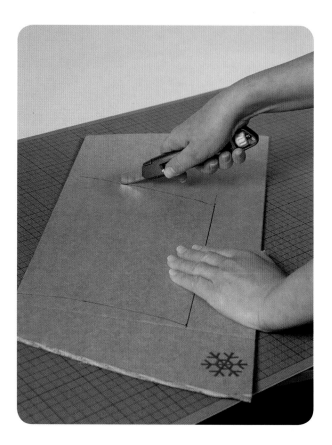

9. Use the glue gun to secure the inside of the back section to the drawer—right on the edge, starting at the bottom then continuing up the sides. For a neater finish, sand down and apply kraft tape to all the inside and outside edges of each drawer (bottom, sides, and top).

11. To attach pulls to the drawers, drill one (or several) holes to match the diameter of the screws on the front of each drawer using a hand drill. Depending on the style of the pulls, screws may be included—if not, make sure you use appropriate screws and flat washers. After placing washers on them, put the threads through the holes, positioning their heads so their points face the front of the drawer, then screw on the pulls.

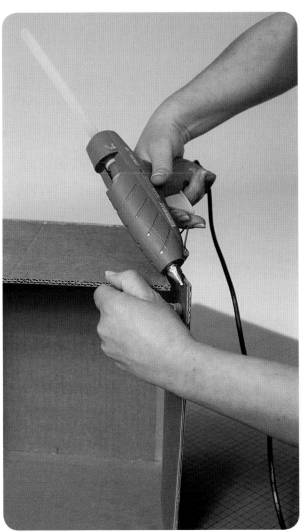

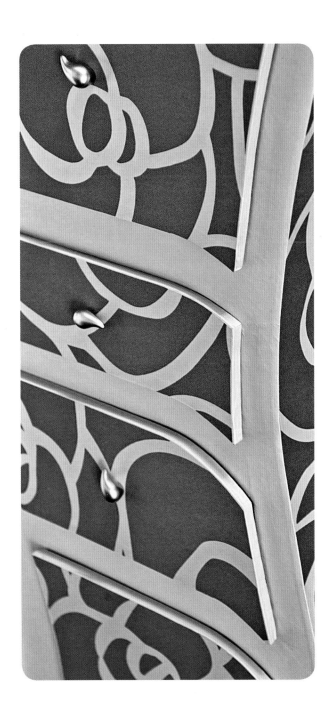

10. Paint your furniture, or cover it with paper, and varnish if necessary (see steps 15, 16, and 17 on pages 16-17).

Boomerang Chair

This very trendy chair can be adapted to a number of styles depending on the choice of covering (paint, decorative paper, faux leather paper, etc.). Here, black paint and natural bamboo sticks create a mellow, stripped-down style.

Materials and Finishing

Cardboard: 6 double-wall sheets, 60 x 90 cm (24 x 35")

Extra double-wall cardboard for crosspieces and covering

Bamboo mat or blind, 3.40 x 0.40 m (11 x 1 3/8')

Tissue paper (or kraft paper)

Black acrylic paint

Wallpaper paste

Wood glue

Colorless, water-based parquet varnish

Paintbrushes

Tools

Cutting mat

Utility knife and blades (18 mm [3/4"])

Hot glue gun and glue sticks

Ruler

Tape measure

Cutting rule

Try square

Jigsaw

Sandpaper (coarse and fine grades)

Sanding block

Roll of kraft tape

Drawing pencil and black marker

Building the Chair

1 With the aid of a ruler, trim the base of each of the 6 cardboard sheets using the utility knife to leave a clean, flat edge, positioning the corrugations vertically.

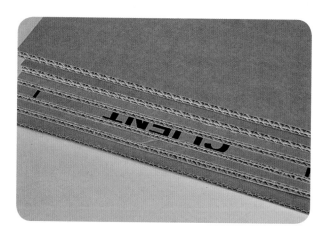 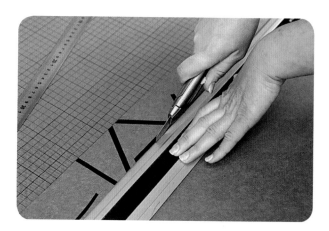

2 Lay the 6 sheets on top of each other, making sure their bases are aligned, and fasten them together with kraft tape so they do not slip during the cutting process.

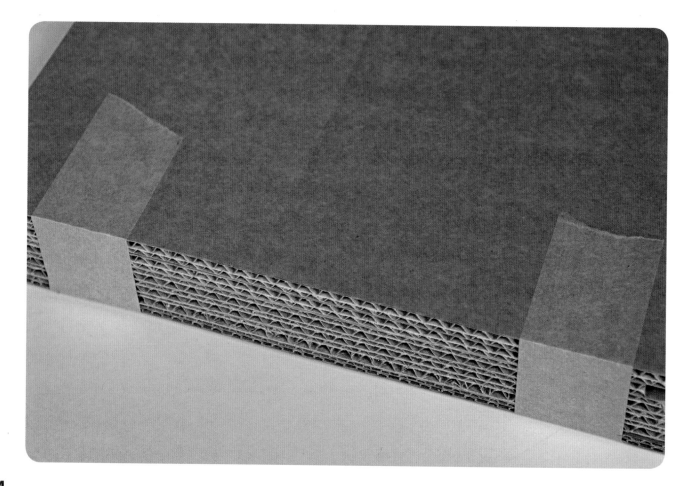

3 With a pencil, draw the outline of the chair on the top sheet of cardboard, following Figure A. Pay particular attention to the curves. Once your outline is complete, go over it again in black marker.

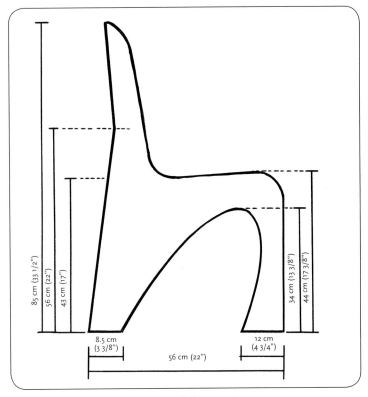

Figure A. General shape and dimensions.

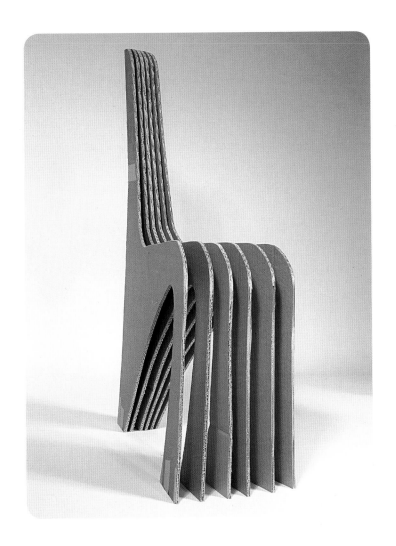

4 Cut around the outline of the chair with the jigsaw, making sure you cut through all 6 sheets. Refasten with kraft tape as you cut so the sheets do not slip. Then, separate the 6 sheets by cutting the kraft tape away and numbering them from 1 (the sheet with the drawing) to 6, paying attention to the order in which you have cut them.

5 Place sheets 1 and 6 (the outer sheets) to one side and lay the other four, one on top of the other, to join them with kraft tape. Once sheets 2, 3, 4, and 5 have been taped together, draw on the top one (now sheet 2) all of the 0.7 cm (1/4") slots, as shown in Figure B. Measure each line pair where indicated on the plan, and make a mark at the middle point to show the cut line of the slot (in black). When two parallel lines slant, calculate the middle point of the shortest line. Each notch therefore has a different length depending on its position.

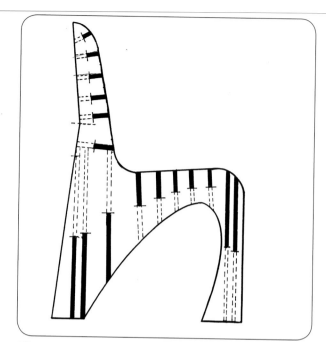

Figure B. Outline of the slots

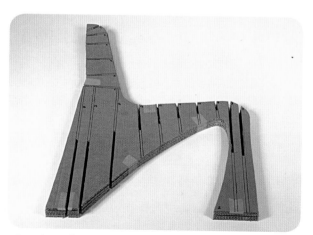

The slots during the cutting process

6 Cut out the slots with the utility knife (along the lines in black marker), cutting through all four sheets at once. Then cut the kraft tape holding the sheets together. Number all of the slots 1 to 16.

7 Place sheet 2 against sheet 6 to pencil on all of the positions for the cut notches. Then, again with the help of sheet 2, pencil the positions of the notches on the back of sheet 1.

8 On double-wall cardboard, draw and cut out the 16 crosspieces (see Figure C). All of them are 38.8 cm (15 1/4") in length and their heights vary according to their position. On each one, draw and cut four slots with the utility knife. The length of each slot will measure half the width of the crosspiece itself and be 0.7 cm (1/4") wide. Number them 1 to 16 according to the slots into which they will be fitted, then fit the crosspieces onto sheets 2, 3, 4, and 5 to form the central structure.

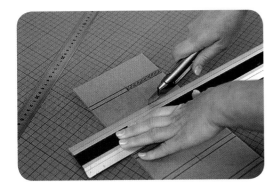

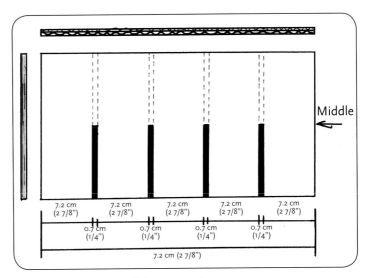

Figure C. Outline of the crosspieces.

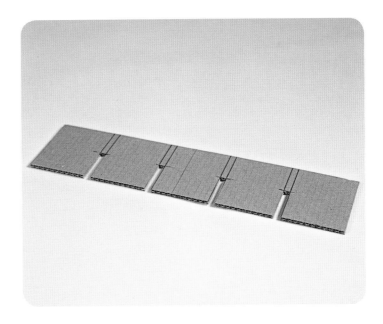

9 Once the crosspieces are fitted, glue the newly formed structure to the outside sheets (sheet 1 and 6) with the glue gun, matching each piece to its respective position. You can use strips of kraft paper in place of the hot glue gun; it is more tedious but a greener option.

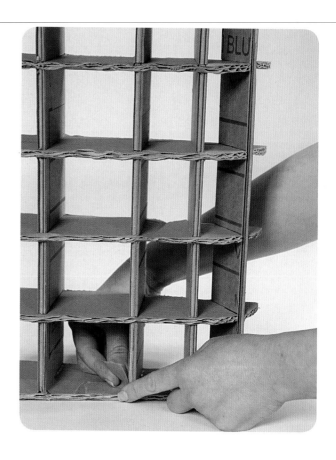

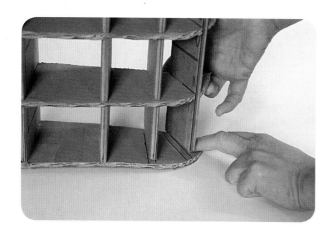

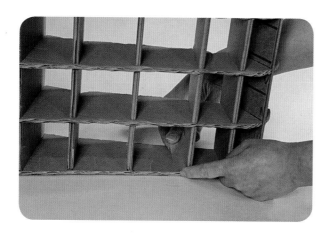

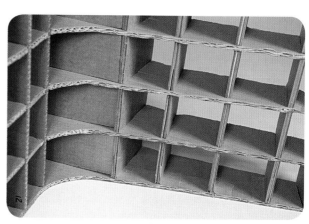

10 To cover the outside, draw and cut out long strips of double-wall cardboard, of equal width to the chair, with the corrugations running sideways so the cardboard curves more easily. To cover the seat, you will have to join several sheets together (see p.8). Be sure to square off the bottom of your sheet.

11 In order to bend the cardboard so that it adopts the curvature of the chair, mold it over the edge of a table or with the help of a tube. Test the sheet regularly so it follows the curvature of the chair perfectly, and be sure to change the direction of the curve as appropriate. Start with the bottom of the feet; continue with the front, the seat and the back, and then with the curve on top. Finish with two sheets of cardboard on the back: the first above the curve for the back, and the second below and down to the feet.

12 To make assembly easier, lay the chair on its side on your work surface for more stability and guidance, keeping it parallel. Glue your molded sheets in the same order as the previous step. With the hot glue gun, start by gluing the two inside edges of the cardboard in sections of about 20 cm (8"), as the glue will set very quickly.

13 Sand down the outside of the chair, starting with the coarse sandpaper and finishing off with the fine. Around the visible corrugations and ridges of the piece, hold your sanding block flat so you don't damage the edges.

14 Remove the dust from the sanding process and stick strips of kraft tape along all the edges of the chair. Place the strips over the corrugations and fold the other half over. On curves, notch the strips with scissors before folding over.

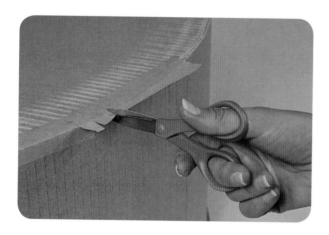

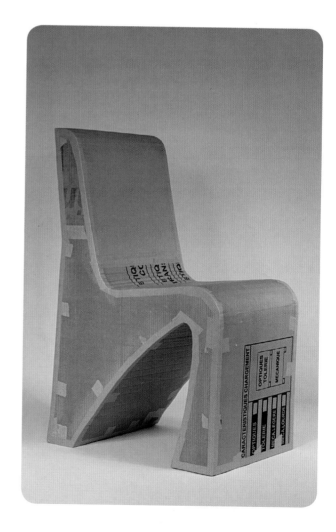

The Finishing Touches

1 Apply two coats of black paint to both sides of the chair, running over the edges slightly with excess. Let the chair dry between each coat.

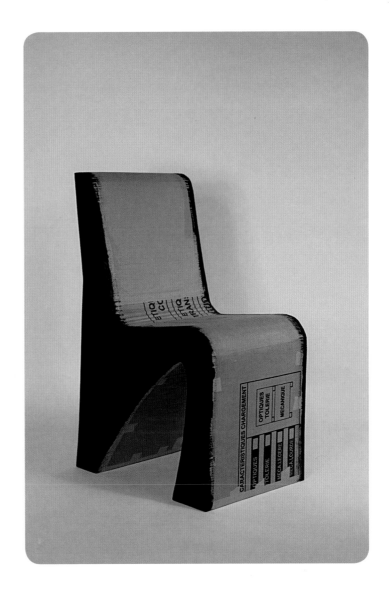

2 On the bamboo mat or blind, measure and draw the width of the chair seat, cutting with the utility knife and removing the fabric binding along the edges. Remember, the bamboo slats must lie across the curvature of the chair. Lightly sand down the cut edges as required.

3 Attach the bamboo panel with wood glue. Start with the lower part of the chair and unroll the bamboo panel upwards, gluing the cardboard surface of the chair to the back of the bamboo panel as you go. Finish at the back of the chair. Also, glue a strip of bamboo to the underside of the seat. If a single panel isn't long enough, put the seam in the groove of the chair or at the back.

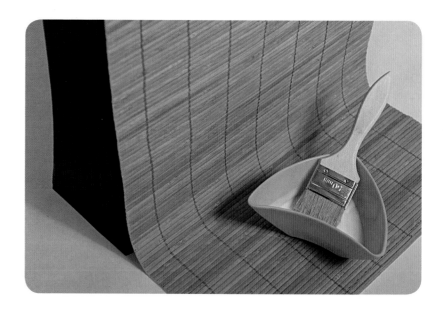

4 Once the glue is completely dry, apply one or two coats of varnish, letting it dry between each.

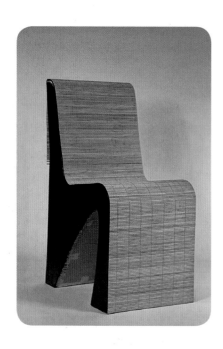

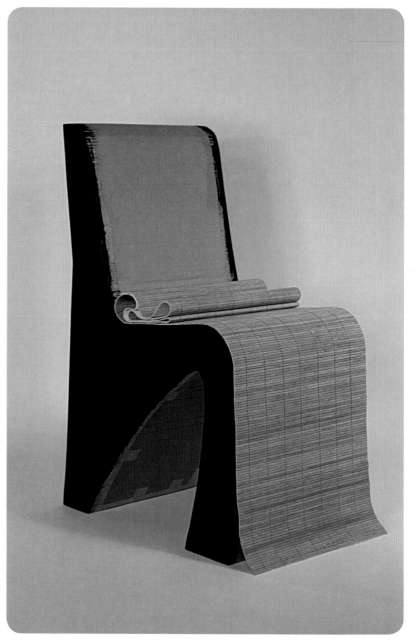

Romantic Console

A subtle mix of baroque shapes and modern tones, this console is ideal in a foyer or dining room, holding a lamp, ornaments, or a butler tray. The rose-patterned paper and matching drawer pulls add a touch of romance.

Materials and finishing

Cardboard: 5 double-wall sheets, 1.40 x 0.95 m (4 5/8 x 3 1/8')

Allow extra cardboard for the crosspieces, the lining of the case, the drawer, and the outside covering

A sheet of grey cardboard (3 mm [1/8"] thick): 1.05 x 0.35 m (3 3/8 x 1 1/8')

A roll of black paper (55 cm [22"] wide): 4 m (13 1/8')

A roll of silver paper (55 cm wide): 5.20 m (17')

A roll of paper with white roses on a black background (55 cm wide): 2.60 m (8 1/2')

Black satin acrylic paint (a small quantity)

Wallpaper paste

White glue

Two white porcelain drawer pulls (rose design), with screws

2 metal washers

Colorless water-based parquet varnish

Paintbrushes

Tools

A cutting mat

Utility knife and blades (18 mm [3/4"])

Hot glue gun and glue sticks

Ruler

Tape measure

Cutting rule

Try square

Jigsaw

Sandpaper (various grades)

Sanding block

Roll of kraft tape

Drawing pencil and black marker

Drill with bit the size of the screws (or hand drill)

Building the Console

1 Trim the base of the five cardboard sheets with the utility knife to leave a clean, flat edge. Position the corrugations vertically, using the try square.

2 Lay the five sheets on top of each other, aligning their cut bases, and fasten them together with kraft tape along the edges so that they do not slip during cutting.

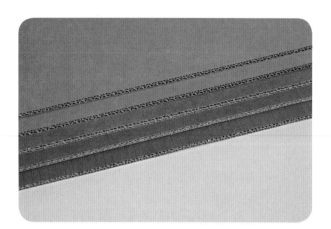

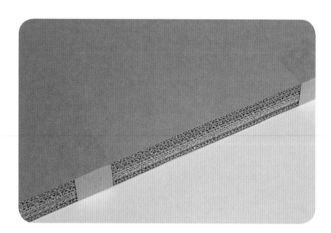

3 Following Figure A, draw the general design of the console on the top sheet, as well as the layout of the lower shelf and that of the inside of the drawer. Once you have done this, go over the lines in black marker.

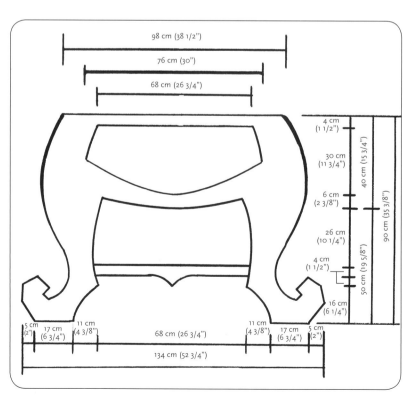

Figure A. General shape and dimensions.

Dimensions shown in Figure A:
98 cm (38 1/2")
76 cm (30")
68 cm (26 3/4")
4 cm (1 1/2")
30 cm (11 3/4")
40 cm (15 3/4")
6 cm (2 3/8")
90 cm (35 3/8")
26 cm (10 1/4")
4 cm (1 1/2")
50 cm (19 5/8")
16 cm (6 1/4")
5 cm (2")
17 cm (6 3/4")
11 cm (4 3/8")
68 cm (26 3/4")
11 cm (4 3/8")
17 cm (6 3/4")
5 cm (2")
134 cm (52 3/4")

4 With the jigsaw, cut out the outlines of the console, as well as the top and bottom of the shelf, making sure you cut through all five sheets. Do not cut the case for the drawer at this stage—you will do that later. Apply kraft tape along the cut edges so the sheets do not slide. Then, sand down all of the cut edges with the sanding block and medium grade sandpaper.

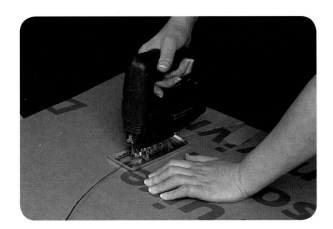

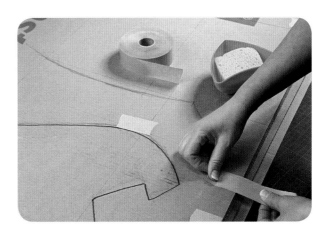

5 Separate the five sheets by cutting the kraft tape with the utility knife. Take away the back sheet (keeping it for the back of the unit) and number it (sheet 5). Then, starting with the front sheet, number the others 1 to 4, ending with the back sheet.

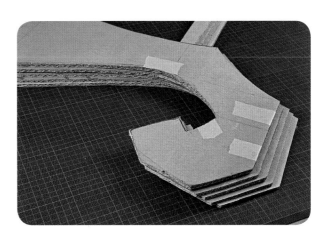

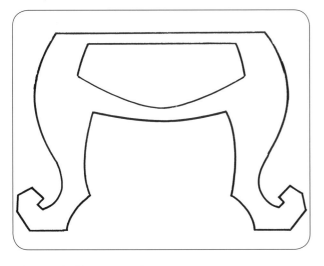

Figure B. Sheet number 1.

6 On sheet number 1, cut out the bottom shelf with the utility knife and remove it, as in Figure B. With the kraft tape, now assemble sheets 1, 2, 3, and 4 to cut out the inside of the drawer with the jigsaw. Save the cut-outs. Lightly sand down all of the sheets to get rid of any excess caused by the cutting process.

7 Separate the sheets and remove sheet 1. With the kraft tape, fasten sheets 2, 3, and 4 together in order to draw on the 0.7 cm (1/4") slots, as shown in Figure C. Cut them with the knife, always to the midpoint (as shown with the solid black lines). Each slot is of a different height, depending on its position. At this stage, you still don't need to draw the bottom shelf slots.

8 Remove sheet 2 and stick sheets 3 and 4 together. Draw the bottom shelf slots on these sheets, as shown in Figure D, and cut them out with the knife, going to the midpoint.

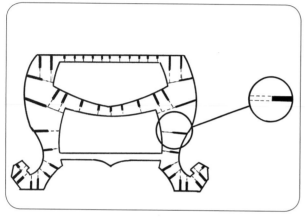

Figure C. Slots on sheets 2, 3, and 4.

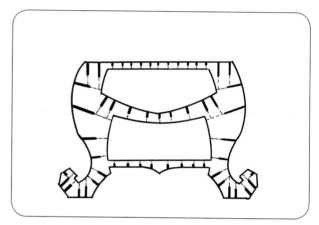

Figure D. Slots on sheets 3 and 4.

9 On double-wall cardboard, draw and cut out the crosspieces with the utility knife. All of them should be 33 cm (15 1/4") long (except those for the shelf, which should be 27.8 cm [11"] long) and their heights will vary depending on where they are positioned. On the longer ones, draw and cut out three 0.7 cm (1/4") wide slots half the height of the crosspieces, and two slots on the shorter pieces for the shelf. As you cut, number each crosspiece and mark its position on the central sheets so that assembling them is easier.

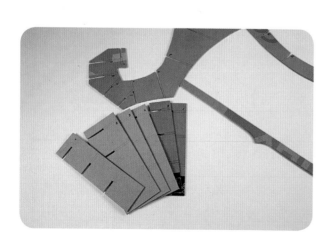

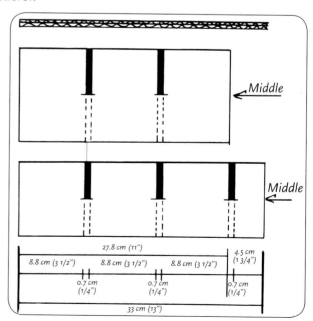

Figure E. The crosspieces.

10 Position sheet 3 (the sheet with all the cut slots) on sheet 5 in order to mark the slots' positions in pencil. Again using sheet 3, mark the positions of the slots on the back of sheets 1 and 2. This will give you reference points when gluing the structure to the front and back sheets.

11 Fasten the longest crosspieces to sheets 2, 3, and 4, using the numbering to guide you, and the shortest crosspieces to sheets 3 and 4 for the shelf. Once the crosspieces are in place, fasten them to sheet 5 (the back sheet) with the glue gun, and then to sheet 1.

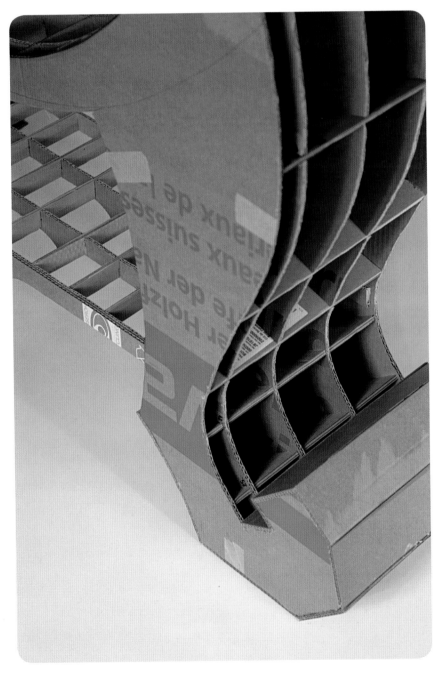

12 To cover the outside of the console, cut out strips of double-wall cardboard with the same width as the depth of the console, laying the corrugations horizontally so the cardboard bends easier. The cardboard will have to go all around the console, so you will have to join several sheets together (see "Joining Sheets of Cardboard," p. 8). Make sure you square off the bottom of each sheet. To bend the cardboard so it follows the curves, mold a sheet over the edge of a table or with the help of a tube (see p. 15 or p. 29).

Fasten the sheets with the glue gun, progressing in sections since the glue sets very quickly. Start at the bottom of the feet. Since these have sharp angles, you will need several pieces of cardboard cut to fit. Continue up the sides, then do the top and the bottom of the shelf. Finally, finish with the top of the console.

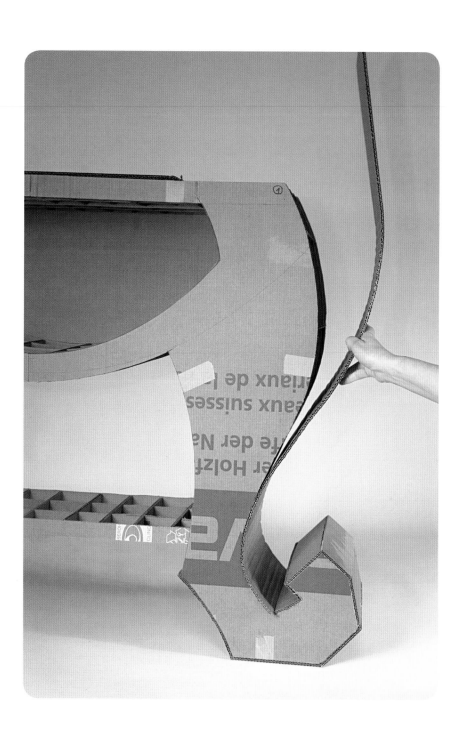

13 On double-wall cardboard, draw and cut out the raised part, which will be placed around the drawer case, following the measurements in Figure F. This raised section will extend 0.7 cm (1/4") past the sides of the console. Then, using the template for the front face of the drawer (set aside in step 6), line it by attaching a piece of double-wall cardboard of the same size. Sand the surfaces of the two sheets and apply kraft tape along the edges. For this, position the strip lengthwise across the edge and fold each side down, notching the tape along the lower curve.

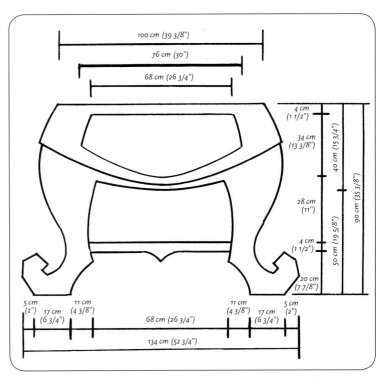

Figure F.

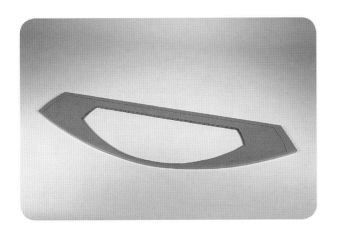

14 With the glue gun, fasten the raised part around the case of the drawer. To position it correctly, use the case as a reference point. Mold, cut, and glue two pieces of double-wall cardboard to the sides of the raised part to complete the 0.7 cm (1/4") overhang at the front.

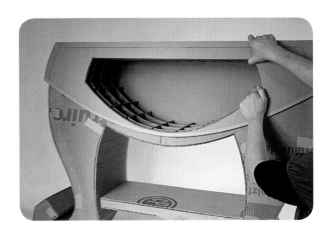

15 Draw and cut out double-wall cardboard to line the case that will hold the drawer. For this, measure the width and then the depth, from the back to the front. Position the visible corrugations towards yourself, facing the front. Start with the bottom of the case, measuring the curve with a tape measure, and then mold your sheet to follow the curve. Glue it to the back with a thin line of hot glue along the back cut edge. Once dry, fasten to the front by depositing a thin line of glue behind the edge of the piece's front face. Continue with the sides and finish with the top, always gluing the back first, then the front. Sand down the entire console.

16 On visible corrugations and ridges, hold your sanding block flat in order not to damage the edges.

17 Remove the dust from the sanding process, and then apply kraft tape over all the visible corrugations, as well as along the inside and outside edges. On curves, place the kraft tape over the corrugations and notch with scissors before folding over.

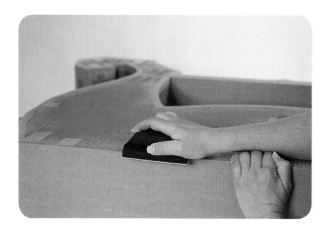

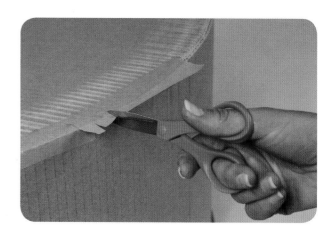

18 To build the drawer, see steps 3 to 9 in the introduction on pages 17-20, bearing in mind that you have already made the front piece in step 13.

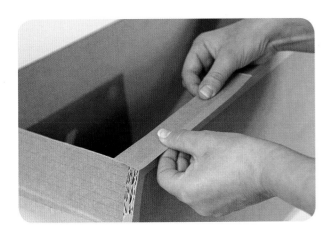 

 19 To reinforce the top of the console so it is strong enough to support objects without perforating the cardboard, draw and cut out a sheet of grey cardboard (3 mm [1/8"] thick) to match the dimensions of the top of the console and apply with white glue.

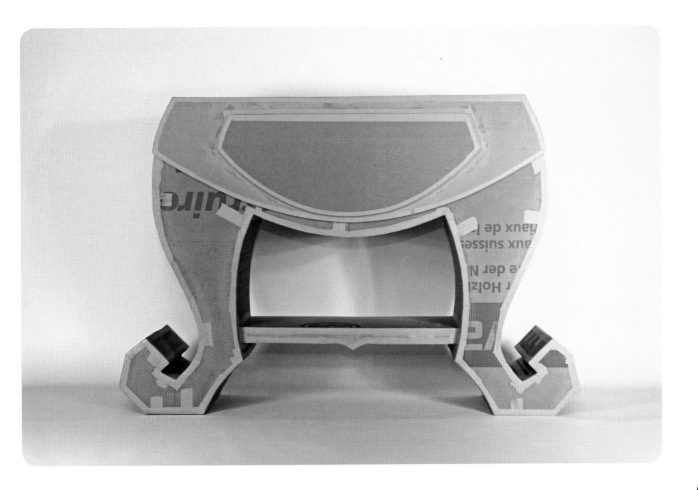

Finishing Touches

Paper

1 With the black satin paint, paint the surface of the lower part of the front and the two sides. You can go over the edges slightly since the paper will eventually cover these areas. Leave to dry.

2 With the wallpaper paste, glue silver paper to the front of the console, leaving a 1 cm (3/8") allowance around the outside. Then fold the extra material over the underside by notching the edges with scissors. Join the paper vertically, putting pieces edge to edge, as we are using plain paper for this part of the design. To keep your seams neat, lay the edges of the paper on top of each other and cut them both together. Get rid of the excess paper: the two edges will meet perfectly. In the same way, cover the outer sides of the console and the feet by gluing on black paper. Lay it flush with the edge of the front side, leaving a 1 cm (3/8") allowance at the back that you can fold behind the console.

3 Cover the interior of the console with silver paper by gluing it flush with the edge of the front side and leaving a 1 cm (3/8") allowance that you can later fold to the back of the console. Now cover the shelf with black paper: start with the facing edge, including a 1 cm (3/8") allowance on either side that you can fold around the shelf. Continue with the surface of the shelf by gluing paper flush with the edge of the front, allowing enough to cover the thickness of the shelf at the back and to finish on its underside with a 1 cm (3/8") allowance. Now glue a strip of paper to the underside of the shelf, flush with all edges.

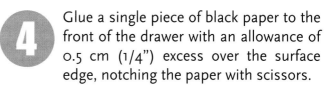

4 Glue a single piece of black paper to the front of the drawer with an allowance of 0.5 cm (1/4") excess over the surface edge, notching the paper with scissors.

5 Stick a strip of black paper (2 cm [3/4"] wide) around the rim of the front of the drawer, positioning it flush with the edge and folding it back after notching with scissors. To finish, apply a strip of kraft tape along the inside facing of the drawer. Cover the bottom of the drawer with silver paper.

6 Glue the patterned paper to the raised section. Start with the front face, gluing the paper flush with the curve and cutting with the knife. Leave an allowance of 1 cm (3/8") that you can fold over the top of the console, as well as on either side. Now, attach a long strip of paper across the width of the console to cover the top and the sides. At the bottom of the sides and along the front, cut flush with the edge, leaving an allowance of 1 cm (3/8") on the part of the strip that will end up at the back (which you can fold over).

Wait for the glue to dry completely, then apply three thin coats of varnish to the entire console, letting it dry between each coat.

Drawer Pulls

Mark the position of the pull on the front of the drawer and drill two holes that match the size of the screws with either an automatic or a hand drill. Under the head of each screw, on the inside of the drawer, position a metal washer so as not to enlarge the perforation. Then screw on the pulls from the outside.

Cube Armchair

The volume of this chair is encapsulated in a cube.
All kinds of variations are possible, depending on the type and color of
the paper with which you cover it.

Materials and Finishing

Cardboard: 8 double-wall sheets,
0.70 x 0.70 m (27 1/2 x 27 1/2")

Allow extra double-wall cardboard for
crosspieces, zigzag reinforcements, and
exterior covering

6 sheets of red Skivertex paper, 65 x 100 cm
(25 1/2 x 39 3/8") (from a specialty arts and
crafts store)

Grey cardboard (3 mm [1/8"] thick): 3
sheets, at least 66 cm (26") wide

White glue

Colorless, water-based parquet varnish

Paintbrush

Tools

Cutting mat

Utility knife and blades (18 mm [3/4"])

Hot glue gun and glue sticks

Ruler

Tape measure

Cutting rule

Try square

Jigsaw

Sandpaper (different grades)

Sanding block

Roll of kraft tape

Drawing pencil and black marker

Building the Chair

1 Trim the base of each of the eight sheets of cardboard with the utility knife to leave a clean, flat edge, aligning corrugations vertically with the help of the try square. Lay the eight sheets on top of each other, aligning their cut bases and positioning the two top sheets to make sure that the sides with the larger corrugations (the back) are facing each other and the sides with the smaller corrugations (the front) are facing out, as shown in Figure A. Do the same for the bottom two sheets. The stronger side of cardboard is the one with smaller corrugation flutes (where text is usually printed). So, the cardboard that will be used for the armrest will have its stronger side facing out and towards the inside of the seat. Once your sheets are in the correct position, fasten them together by applying kraft tape to the perimeter so that they do not slip during cutting.

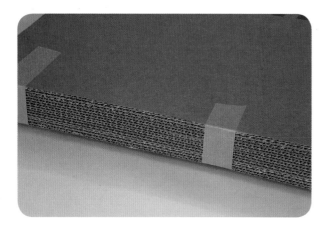

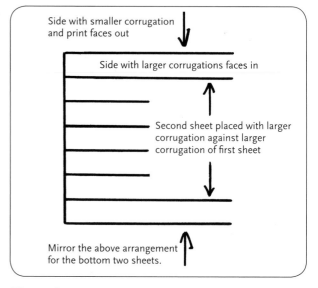

Side with smaller corrugation and print faces out

Side with larger corrugations faces in

Second sheet placed with larger corrugation against larger corrugation of first sheet

Mirror the above arrangement for the bottom two sheets.

Figure A.

2 On the top sheet, draw the outside outline of the armchair with a pencil, following Figure B and making sure everything is kept square. Then draw the rounded edge, making an arc with a radius equal to 6.5 cm (2 1/2"). Once your lines are final, go over them again in black marker.

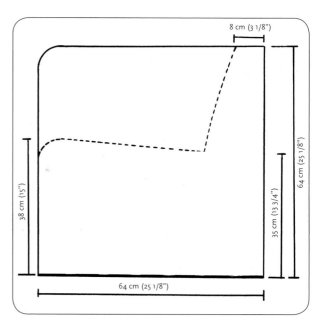

8 cm (3 1/8")

38 cm (15")

35 cm (13 3/4")

64 cm (25 1/8")

64 cm (25 1/8")

Figure B.

3 Cut out the outline of the chair with the jigsaw, making sure you cut through all eight sheets. Reapply kraft tape as you cut so that the sheets do not slide. Lightly sand down the cut edges.

4 Separate the eight sheets by cutting the kraft tape away with a knife and number the sheets 1 to 8, following the order in which they were layered during the cutting process. Put sheets 1, 2, 7, and 8 to one side, then lay the other four together (sheets 3, 4, 5, and 6) and re-assemble them with kraft tape.

5 On the new top sheet (now sheet 3), draw the design of the seat in pencil, following Figure C. Once your lines are final, go over them in black marker.
Cut through all four sheets following your new lines with the jigsaw. Reapply kraft tape as you cut so the sheets do not slide.

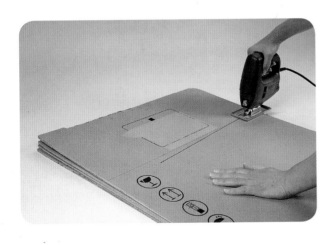

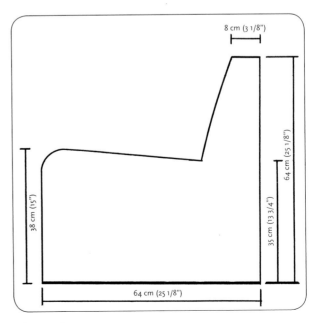

8 cm (3 1/8")

38 cm (15")

35 cm (13 3/4")

64 cm (25 1/8")

64 cm (25 1/8")

Figure C.

6 On sheets 3, 4, 5, and 6 that are fastened together, draw all of the 0.7 cm (1/4") slots as shown in Figure D. Cut them out with the utility knife, up to the midpoint (drawn in black on Figure D). Label them A to F according to the Figure.

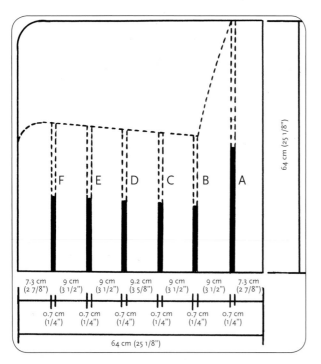

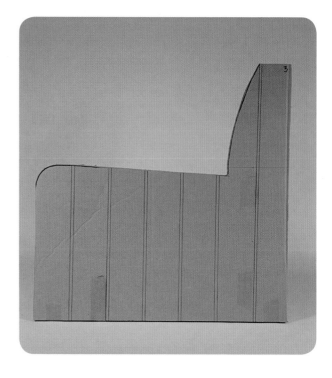

Figure D. Outline of the slots.

7 Separate the sheets. Attach sheets 2 and 7 together with kraft tape and draw the same slot marks, using sheet 3 as a guide. Cut them with the utility knife, as done before.

8 Using double-wall cardboard (with the corrugations placed vertically), draw and cut out the crosspieces. They should all be 64 cm (25 1/4") long and their height will vary depending on their position, since the seat is slightly slanted towards the back. Label them from A to F, following their position on the sheets. Crosspiece A (which will be fitted to the back of the chair) will be the only one measuring the whole height of the chair (64 cm [25 1/4"]). On each of them, draw and cut six slots that go to the midpoint of the crosspiece and are 0.7 cm (1/4") wide.

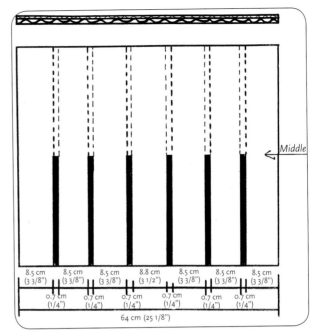

Figure E. The crosspieces.

9 Fit the crosspieces together on sheets 2 to 7, keeping them in the correct order according to the letters.

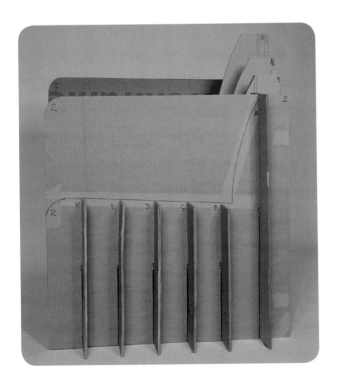

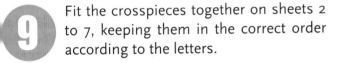

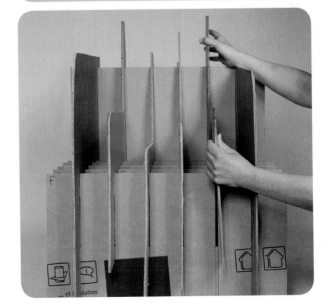

10 Using double-wall cardboard, cut strips 8.5 cm (3 3/8") wide (corresponding to the inner width of each arm) and fold them into zigzag shapes. These strips will strengthen the arms.

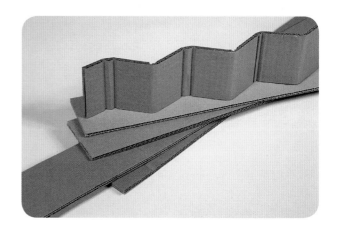

11 Apply hot glue to the edges of the strips and glue them in a zigzag on sheets 2 and 7. Start with the edges, curving the zigzags around the corners: continue by filling the spaces between crosspieces, and finish with the spaces without crosspieces, using strips folded into a more loose zigzag shape.

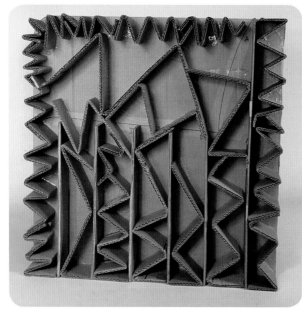

12 Glue the outside sheets (sheets 1 and 8) on either side of the chair, applying thin lines of glue to the edges of the crosspieces and the zigzags.

Once the side sheets are glued, measure and cut a sheet to the dimensions of the bottom of the chair and another sheet to fit the back of the chair. Secure them with the glue gun.

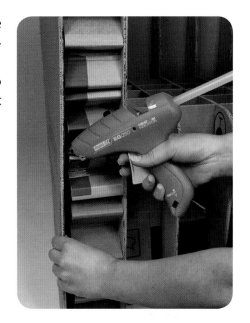

13 Cut and glue cardboard rectangles between the crosspieces of the upper back section to strengthen the chair. To strengthen the sides of the back of the chair (before covering, to make the assembly easier), take two pieces of tri-wall cardboard (or two layers of double-wall cardboard), and mark them to fit the chair back. Cut them out with the knife.

14 Hot-glue these curved reinforcements to each side of the back, against sheets 2 and 7.

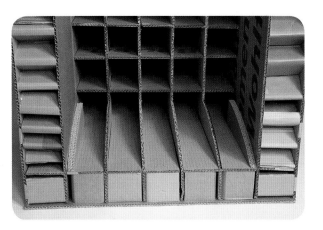

15 To cover the back of the chair, cut a sheet of double-wall cardboard, positioning the corrugations horizontally so that they follow the curvature of the back of the chair. This strip must be the exact width and height as the back section. Use a tape measure to calculate the curvature at the back of the chair. Mold before fastening (see p. 15 or p. 29) and check that it is squared off. When gluing it, start at the base, continue with the sides, and finish with the top.

16 Following the same method used for the back reinforcements (steps 13 and 14), strengthen the rounded edge of the seat so you can attach a covering later on.

17 To cover the seat and arms, cut a sheet of double-wall cardboard the same width as the chair, positioning the corrugations horizontally so that they follow the chair's curvature. The sheet must be squared off and long enough to cover the seat, the arms, and the front of the chair; if not, you will have to combine sheets (see p. 8). If combining, do not put the seam on the curve, but rather on the flat part of the chair. To calculate the height, lay your sheet along the front of the chair, starting with its bottom edge flush to the base. Make a reference point with a pencil to mark the height at which you will cut the arm rests. The cardboard must be squared off to fit perfectly and to cover the arms entirely (except in the case of a combined piece).

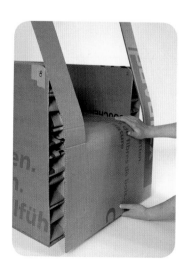

18 Put the chair on its side so that your work table can be used as a guide. With the glue gun, start by gluing about 30 cm (11 7/8") of one side, then glue 30 cm (11 7/8") of the other side. Continue this way to the back of the seat and the arms.

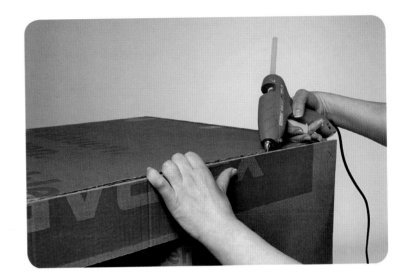

19 Sand down all corrugations and edges, placing your sanding block flat so as not to damage them. Start with the coarser sandpaper and finish with the finer. Remove the dust from the sanding process, and apply strips of kraft tape along the edges and visible corrugations of the cardboard. On curves, apply kraft tape along the corrugations, notching with scissors before folding down.

20 To prevent the cardboard's corrugation from crushing, draw and cut some grey cardboard (3 mm [1/8"] thick) as in step 17. Mold and secure it into position to cover the seat, arms, and front of the chair.

Finishing Touches

1 On two sheets of Skivertex, draw and cut out the covering for the sides of the chair: include a 0.5 cm (1/4") allowance along three of the edges (the top and the sides) as well as 3 cm (1 1/8") extra that you will tuck underneath the chair.

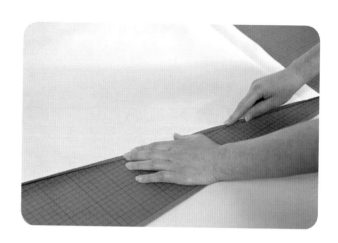

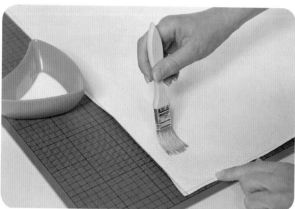

2 Cover one side of the armchair and the sheet of paper with the white glue and place the Skivertex.

Fold over the excess and glue it down, using a small paintbrush. Cut the corner with scissors to follow the curve of the armrest, leaving a 0.5 cm (1/4") allowance.

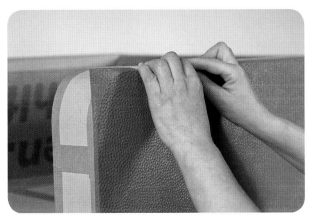

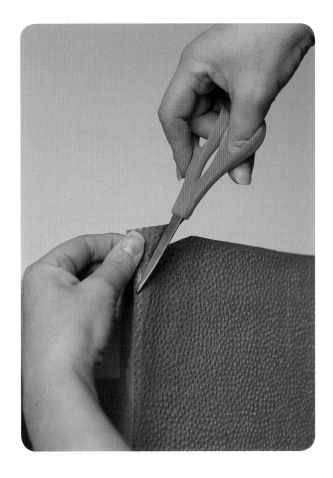

 Notch the curve of the armrest with scissors in order to glue it down.

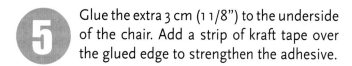

5 Glue the extra 3 cm (1 1/8") to the underside of the chair. Add a strip of kraft tape over the glued edge to strengthen the adhesive.

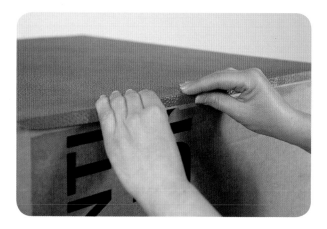

6 Using the same method, repeat on the other side of the chair.

7 To cover the inside of the chair, start by positioning the paper to mark the folds with your finger. Cut the sheet, leaving a 0.5 cm (1/4") allowance on all sides. Test your cutting and adjust as required so that the extra length is no more than 0.5 cm (1/4"). Then, fasten it down using the white glue, folding it in at the sides and notching it on the curves.

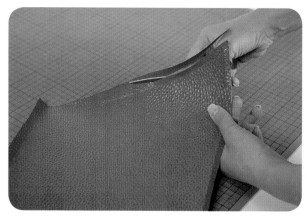

8 Cut the seat, the arms, and the front face of the chair from one sheet of paper. Just as you cut the cardboard in step 17, calculate the exact width, without allowance. For the length, allow 3 cm (1 1/8") extra to tuck underneath the chair. If one sheet of Skivertex isn't enough, you will have to combine materials at the height of the armrests. To keep your work neat, align the edges of the paper and cut through both at the same time. Get rid of the excess paper: the two edges will join perfectly. Cover the back section of the chair by cutting the exact width, but with an allowance of 0.5 cm (1/4") at the top of the sheet that you can fold over.

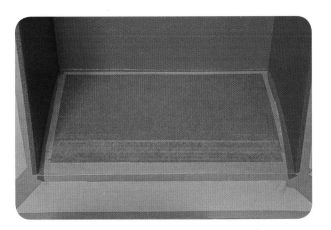 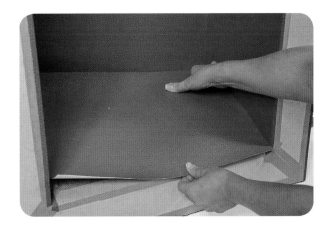

9 To finish, cut three strips of paper (no allowance) to cover the two arms and the back section. Let it dry for 24 hours so the water in the glue evaporates completely.

10 Once the glue has completely set, varnish the whole chair with two thin coats, letting it dry between each coat. You can then accessorize the chair with a matching cushion.

Designer Coffee Table

This contemporary coffee table has a few tricks up its sleeve!
The cardboard is hidden under a faux, raw cement finish. A side case and
a magazine rack complete this sleek piece.

Materials and Finishing

Cardboard: 5 double-wall sheets, 47 x 102 cm (18 1/2 x 40")

Allow extra double-wall cardboard for crosspieces, case linings, and exterior covering

White, matte acrylic paint

Black coloring/dye

Paste wax

Large sponge to apply wax

Filler and a spackle knife

Talcum powder

Colorless, water-based parquet sealant

Paintbrush

Tools

Cutting mat

Utility knife and blades (18 mm [3/4"])

Hot glue gun and glue sticks

Ruler

Tape measure

Cutting rule

Try square

Jigsaw

Sandpaper (medium and fine grades)

Sanding block

Roll of kraft tape (3.5 cm [1 3/8"] wide)

Drawing pencil and black marker

Building the Table

1 Trim the base of each of the five sheets of cardboard with the utility knife to leave a clean, flat edge, aligning corrugations vertically with the help of the try square. Lay the five sheets on top of each other by lining up their cut bases, and fasten them together with kraft tape so they do not slip during cutting.

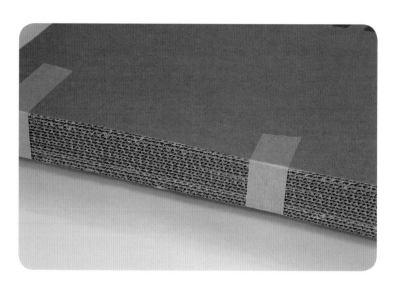

2 On the top sheet, draw the four diagonal lines with a pencil, as shown on Figure A. Then draw the rounded corners with an arc that has a radius of 3.5 cm (1 3/8"). Once your lines are final, go over them in black marker.

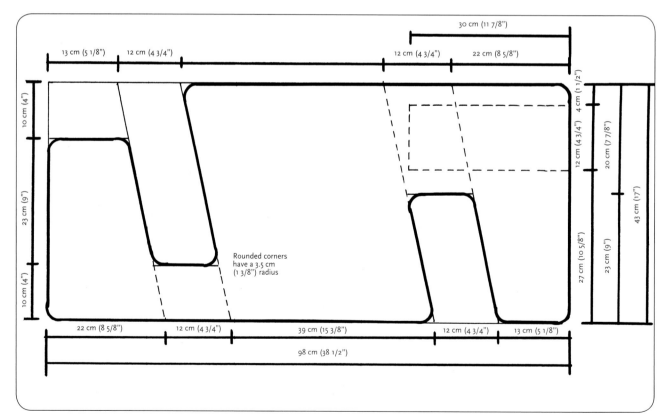

Figure A. General shape and dimensions.

3 Cut around the outline with the jigsaw, making sure you cut through all five sheets. Reapply kraft tape as you cut so the sheets do not slip. Lightly sand down these cut edges.

4 Separate the five sheets by cutting the kraft tape away, and number them 1 to 5. Put sheets 1 and 5 (the outer sheets) to one side, then align the other three and fasten them together with kraft tape.

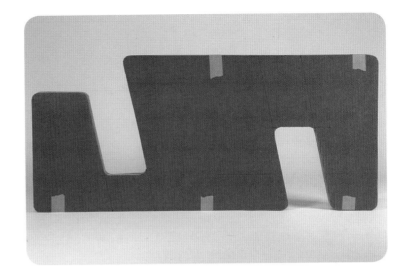

5 On the top sheet (sheet 2), draw the case as well as all the 0.5 cm (1/4") wide slots, as shown on Figure B. Cut the case with the jigsaw, and the slots with the utility knife to their midpoint (the solid black lines). Each slot has a different length depending on its position.

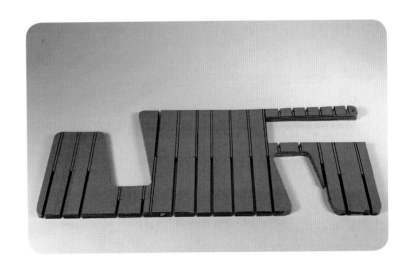

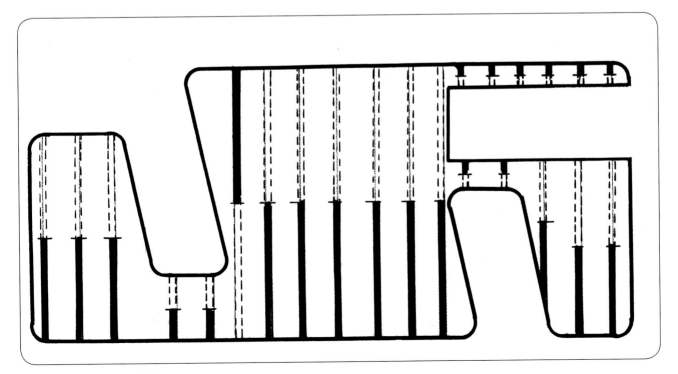

Figure B. Outline of the slots.

6 Separate the three sheets by cutting the kraft tape away with a knife. Put sheet 2 against sheet 5 as a guide to mark all the positions of the cut slots in pencil. Then, still using sheet 2, draw the positions of the slots on to the back of sheet 1.

7 On double-wall cardboard, draw and cut out the 23 cross-pieces. All of them should measure 42.9 cm (16 7/8") long; their heights will vary depending on their position. On each one, draw and cut three 0.7 cm (1/4") wide slots half as high as the crosspiece. Fit all of the crosspieces on sheets 2, 3 and 4.

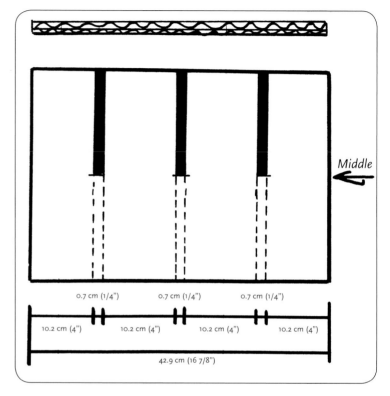

Middle

0.7 cm (1/4")   0.7 cm (1/4")   0.7 cm (1/4")

10.2 cm (4")   10.2 cm (4")   10.2 cm (4")   10.2 cm (4")

42.9 cm (16 7/8")

Figure C. Outline of the slots.

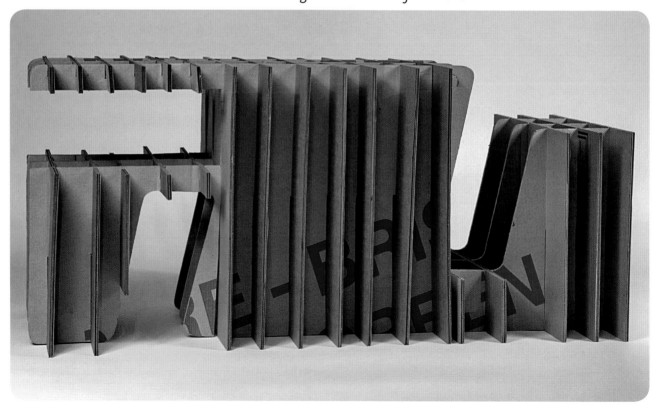

8 Once you have fitted the crosspieces, glue the structure to the outer sheets (sheets 1 and 5), matching the lines to the slots.

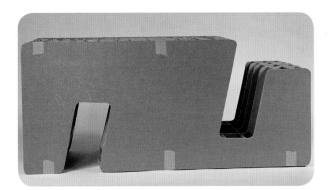

9 On double wall cardboard (with the corrugations positioned vertically), cut the sheets for the lining of the nook. Start with the top and the bottom sheets for the nook by measuring the width, and then the depth, from the back of the case to the edge of the center sheets (sheets 2 to 4). Position the visible corrugations so they face you. Apply them by putting a thin line of glue on the back edge of the sheet; once dry, glue the front edge on top of the crosspieces. Continue by gluing a vertical sheet at the back of the case, between the top and bottom sheet, for the back wall of the nook. Finish with the side sheets: glue three together on each side for reinforcement.

10 Cover the outside of the table with strips of double-wall cardboard the same width as the table, positioning the corrugations at the front so that the cardboard bends more easily. You will need to join several sheets together (see "Joining Sheets of Cardboard," p. 8). Consider molding the cardboard before securing it so that the sheets take on the curves. By covering the exterior of the table, you will also cover the inside of the magazine rack. Test your sheets before gluing to make sure that they are all squared off. Hot-glue the inside edges of the outside sheets, working in sections because the glue will set very quickly.

11 Sand down all of the corrugations and the curves, keeping your sanding block flat to avoid damage. Start with medium grade sandpaper and finish with fine.

Finishing Touches

1 With a spackle knife, coat the entire table with filler paste. Let dry and sand. Apply a second coat, let dry, and sand down again.

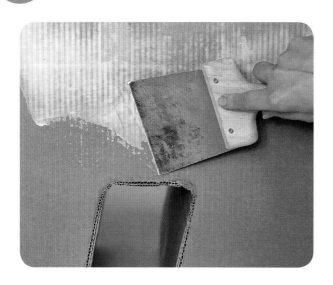

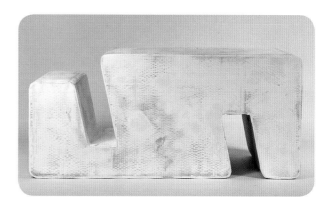

2 Apply two coats of white paint, letting it dry between each coat.

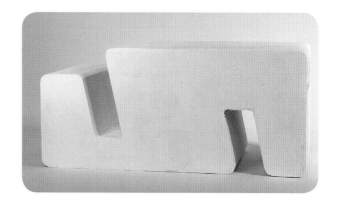

3 Prepare the stain for the table by mixing two tablespoons of wax and a few drops of black dye together in a container. It is entirely up to you how much dye you want to use.

4 With the large sponge, spread the mixture by patting the sponge all over the table in a circular motion. Continue until you have a color that you are happy with. Feel free to make it darker, as the last step tends to fade the color.

5 Powder the whole table in talc and spread it with your hands over the entire surface, so it is applied everywhere. Leave to dry for one day.

6 After drying, remove excess talc with a paintbrush or duster. To finish, apply two thin coats of sealant. Let dry between coats.

Giraffe-shaped Chest of Drawers

This chest of drawers will delight children. With many clever drawers and a neck made of shelves, this giraffe can store all kinds of things in one room. Its colors will appeal to both boys and girls and you will discover that even the eye holds a little secret...

Materials and Finishing

Cardboard: 5 double-wall sheets, 1.82 x 1.85 m (6 x 6')*

Additional double-wall cardboard for crosspieces, case and drawer linings, and exterior covering

Tissue or kraft paper

Acrylic satin paint: raspberry, lime green, black, white, and gold

Wooden dowel (broom handle)

Wallpaper paste

Colorless water-based sealant (optional)

Paintbrush

*You may find it hard to obtain sheets of this size. If so, join the sheets (see p. 8), positioning corrugations perpendicular to the ground. You can also make the giraffe (which stands 1.82 m [6'] tall) smaller by halving the dimensions.

Tools

Cutting mat

Utility knife and blades (18 mm [3/4"])

Hot glue gun and glue sticks

Ruler

Tape measure

Cutting rule

Try square

Jigsaw

Wood saw

Sandpaper (medium and fine grades)

Sanding block

Roll of kraft tape

Drawing pencil and black marker

9 screws and 9 metal washers

Screwdriver

Drill and drill bit to fit screws

Building the Giraffe

1 Trim the base of each of the five sheets of cardboard with the utility knife to leave a clean, flat edge, aligning corrugations vertically with the help of the try square. Arrange the sheets so that the height of the giraffe will run along the longer side of the cardboard.

2 Lay the five sheets of cardboard on top of each other, aligning their cut bases and fastening them together with kraft tape along the perimeter so that they do not slip during cutting.

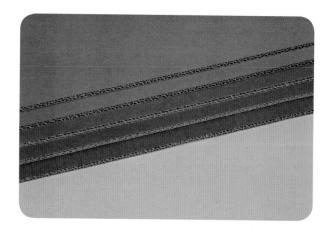

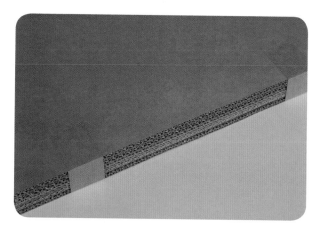

3 Following Figure A, draw the general design of the giraffe on the top sheet, as well as the layout of the drawers, the outside lines (the dotted lines) that correspond to the drawer fronts, and the giraffe's eye (23 cm [9"] in diameter). Once your lines are final, go over them in black marker. The position of the shelving in the neck section will be drawn later on sheet number 2, when the cases are cut.

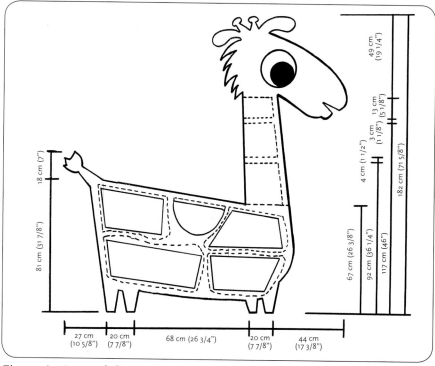

Figure A. General dimensions.

4 Cut around the outline of the giraffe with the jigsaw, making sure you cut through all five sheets. Stick kraft tape along the cut edges so that the sheets do not slip. Lightly sand down all the cut edges.

 6 Put the back sheet to one side (we are keeping this for the back of the unit) and number it (sheet 5). Then number the other four sheets 1 to 4, from front to back.

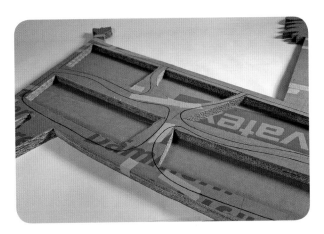

The cut out drawers on sheets 1 to 4, positioned on top of the back sheet (sheet 5).

5 Now fasten sheets 1, 2, 3, and 4 together with kraft tape. With the jigsaw, cut around the outlines of the drawers as well as the eye of the giraffe.

7 Lightly sand down all of these sheets to get rid of any excess material left on the cardboard from the cutting process.

8 Using the tissue paper, trace the front of each drawer (the dotted lines on Figure A) and their inside lines (the full lines) as laid out on sheet 1. Put these tracings to one side. Through the transparency of the paper, the exterior line will be your template for cutting the front of the drawer and will allow you to assemble the drawer against the same front sheet.

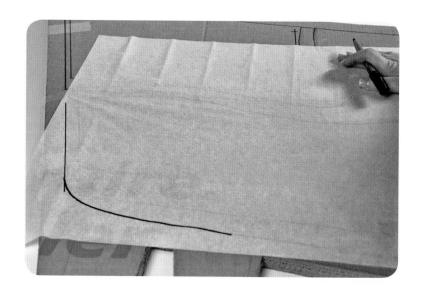

9 Separate the sheets again and put numbers 1 and 5 to one side. Attach the center sheets (sheets 2, 3, and 4) with kraft tape. Following the dimensions in Figure B, draw the lines that will be cut for the shelving in the neck of the giraffe on sheet number 2. These must be parallel and horizontal to the ground. To find the horizontal, use the giraffe's front feet as a guide. Then cut the inside of the shelves with the jigsaw.

Figure B. Slots in the neck.

10 Continue to work on the sheets that we've fastened together (sheets 2, 3, and 4). Draw all the slots with a width of 0.7 cm (1/4"), as shown on Figure C, and cut them out, going to the midpoints (as indicated by the solid black lines). Each slot has a different height depending on its position. Be careful of how weak the neck is at this stage.

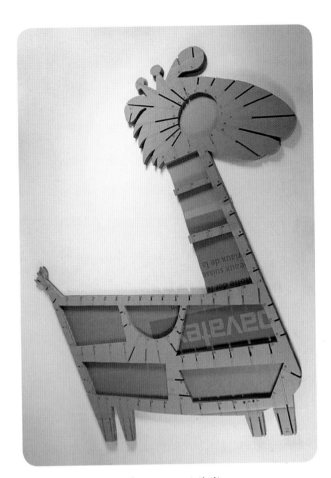

The cut-out slots on sheets 2, 3, and 4, positioned on top of the back sheet for more visibility.

Figure C. The slots.

11 Place sheet 5 (the back sheet) on the work surface and put sheet 2 on top. On sheet 5, draw the positions of the cut slots in pencil. With the help of sheet 2, repeat this process on the back of sheet 1.

12 On double-wall cardboard, draw and cut out the crosspieces. All of them will be 37.9 cm (15") long and their height will vary depending on their position. On each of them, draw and cut three 0.7 cm (1/4") wide slots, going to the midpoint of the crosspiece. Once cut, number each cross section as well as its position on the central sheets. Doing this makes the assembly of the structure easier.

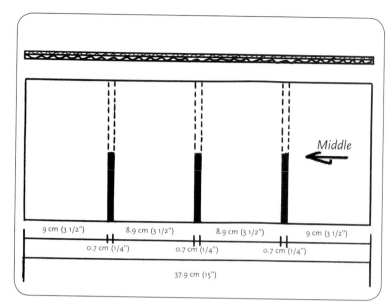

Figure D. The crosspieces.

13 Fit all of the crosspieces together on to sheets 2, 3, and 4, using the numbering system as guidance. Once the crosspieces have been fitted, hot-glue them to sheet number 5 (the back sheet), then to sheet 1 (the front facing).

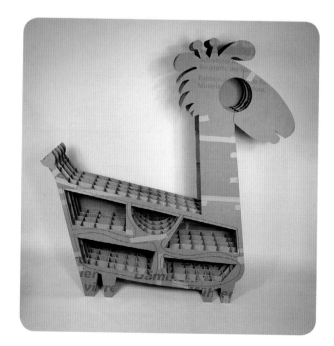

On double-wall cardboard, measure (see the "Introduction," page 15, step 11) and cut the sheets to strengthen the sides of the shelves in the giraffe's neck. Stick three pieces together, alternating the direction of the corrugations of one sheet to another in order to properly strengthen the structure.

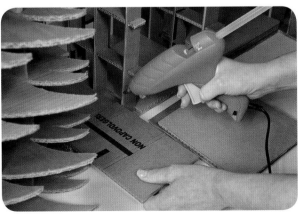

Do the same thing for the top and the bottom of the shelving cases, using a single sheet of cardboard instead of three, and positioning the corrugations towards you, facing front.

 Still using double-wall cardboard, measure, cut, and glue the back of the shelving cases, laying the corrugations so they are vertical when the unit is upright.

 To complete the shelves, cover each of their surfaces by attaching a piece of double-wall cardboard down with the glue gun.

18 Draw and cut out sheets of double-wall cardboard to line the inside of the five cases that will hold the drawers. To do this, measure their width and their depth, from the back up to the front facing sheet. Place the visible corrugations towards you, facing front. Start with the top and the bottom of the cases. Each sheet must be perfectly aligned so as to not leave any space in the corners. Secure them in place with a thin line of glue on the back cut edge of the sheet; once dry, fasten the front edge with a line of glue on the back side of the front facing.

For the half-moon case and the eye, mold your double-wall cardboard, shaping it before gluing. This cardboard must match the frame of each case. In the same way, secure the back sheet first, then the front one.

19 Carry on in the same way to cut and glue sheets for the inside of the cases (except those that are rounded).

20 To cover the outside of the drawers, draw and cut out long strips of double-wall cardboard equal to the depth of the unit. Start by gluing it under the feet of the giraffe, then over the sides of the unit, finishing up at the top (see "Introduction," p. 15, step 12). Place the corrugations facing front so that the cardboard bends more easily, and make the necessary seams following the instructions on page 8.

21 Sand down all of the corrugations of the unit (the front and back edges), starting with the coarse sandpaper and finishing off with the fine. Remove the dust from the sanding process. Now apply strips of kraft tape along all the exposed corrugations as well as along the inside and outside edges of the cases.
On curves, apply kraft tape along the corrugations and notch with scissors before folding and sticking down.

The Drawers

1 Cut sheets of double-wall cardboard and cover the back and the two lateral sides of the four drawer compartments in the shape of a parallelogram (see "Introduction," pgs. 17-18, steps 2-5). For the half-moon-shaped drawer, mold a strip of cardboard with a length that can be adjusted to line the surfaces of the upper interior of the case.

2 For the drawer fronts, use the tracings that we previously made in step 8. For each front, position the tracing paper on double-wall cardboard so it matches the outer line tracings. Be sure corrugations are vertical. Cut each facing and reinforce it by gluing an identical piece of cardboard to the back of it. You can glue these two sheets of cardboard together before marking the outline of the facade so you only cut once with the saw. Sand down the surfaces and apply kraft tape along the outside, positioning the tape over the surface and folding it on each side. Notch with scissors for curves.

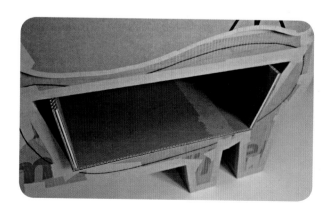

3 On the back of each drawer front, center the paper guide for the interior outlines, as done in step 8, and mark on the inside line of the case.

4 It is not easy to glue the drawer block (bottom and sides) to the front sheet all in one go. Start by gluing the back to the corresponding line, and try to slide each drawer (as a test) into its respective case first to check the positioning. Then, once the glue has lightly set, glue each side.

5 To finish, draw and cut the back panel for each drawer. To do this, place the drawer on double-wall cardboard and draw the inside lines. Then draw a straight line to connect the two lengths of the sides. Cut and glue the back section (see "Introduction," p. 20, steps 8 and 9). For a neater finish, sand and apply kraft tape to all of the edges on each drawer (bottom, sides, and top).

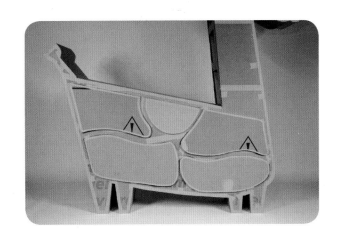

The "Eye" Drawer

1 To make the drawer that is concealed in the giraffe's eye, start by drawing the outline for it with a compass on double-wall cardboard. Two disks, each with a diameter of 23 cm (9"), are required. Cut them out and glue them together with the glue gun. These two disks will be used for the front of the drawer. Then, draw and cut out a disk with a diameter of 10 cm (4") for the pupil. Stick a strip of kraft tape along the outside of each disk to conceal the corrugations, notching the edges with scissors and folding them over.

2 To prevent the drawer from tipping, glue two strips of cardboard 2 cm (3/4") wide to the side of the case that we've already made. Then, for the drawer itself, cut and mold a strip of cardboard of the same length as the circular arc of the drawer that lies below the two strips that we've just fitted, making sure that the depth is the same as the case.

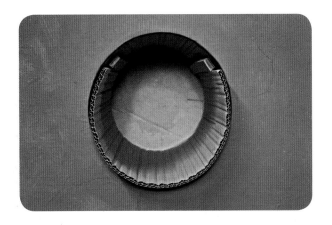

3 On the back of the two disks that are stuck together—that is to say, on the back of the facing—draw a line 0.7 cm (1/4") from the edge along the inner perimeter with a compass. Then hot-glue the drawer within this line.

Place the drawer on the cardboard and draw the back section of the drawer along the inner outlines. Cut and glue it. The pupil will be glued to the facade later, once it has been painted.

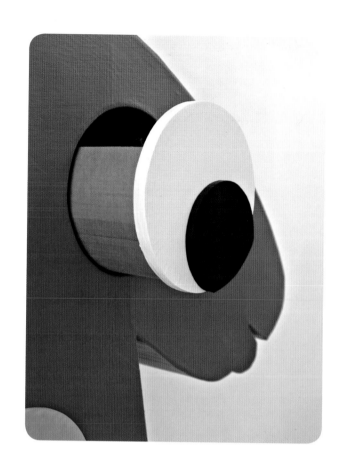

4 To create the giraffe's spots, draw and cut out six disks (23 cm [9"] in diameter) from double-wall cardboard. Leave one whole, and cut the others. Also, cut the shape for the spot that will be used on the neck of the giraffe. Sand and apply kraft tape along the perimeter of the circles and on the spot to cover the corrugations.

Finishing Touches

Painting the Giraffe

1 Tear off pieces of white tissue paper. Tearing the edges is better than cutting with scissors so that the cut lines do not appear under the paint. Apply them with wallpaper paste, making sure you cover the entire giraffe and slightly overlap the tissue paper so it doesn't leave any cardboard visible. Cover the front of the drawers, the spots, and the pupil in the same way. Let it dry so that the water in the paste fully evaporates from the cardboard. This process is needed to prep for painting the surface.

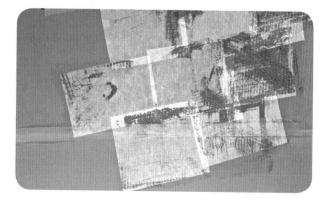

2 Paint the giraffe's body (except the folds of the mane), the fronts of the drawers, and the spot on the neck first, in raspberry. Let dry and paint the round spots, the folds of the mane, and the flat part of the shelving in lime green, then paint the eye in white and the pupil in black. Let dry. Once it is all dry, finish by painting the finer details in gold: the tail, the feet, and the horns. You can now hot-glue the pupil to the eye and the different spots to the front of the drawers and the neck. Depending on the quality of the paint, it is up to you whether you want to apply sealant or not.

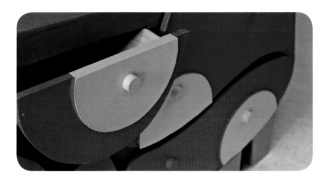

The Drawer Pulls

1 Using the wood saw, cut nine wooden disks, 1.5 cm (5/8") thick from the broom handle. With the drill fitted with a bit the same diameter as the screw, drill a hole in the center of the back of the pulls, making sure you only drill half way through. Paint the pulls in either lime green or raspberry and leave to dry.

2 Mark the position of the pulls in pencil (there are two pulls on the big drawers) and pierce a hole through each mark. After fitting a washer, put the screws through the holes, positioning the heads of the screws to the back of the facade and points towards the front, then screw on each pull.

Tip

If you do not have any metal washers, substitute little squares (3 x 3 cm [1 1/8 x 1 1/8"]) of 3 mm (1/8") plywood.

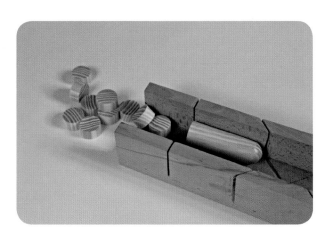

Matching Stools

These little stools accompany the giraffe and are simple to make. You can leave them in the other rooms of the house where they will be perfect as extra seating options. You can also choose a different covering than faux fur: plain fabric, patterned fabric, or painted effects... anything goes!

Materials and Finishing

Cardboard: 1 double-wall sheet, 1 x 1 m
(3 1/4 x 3 1/4')

Cardboard tubes (diameter 6 cm [2 3/8"]):
about 12 x 30 cm (4 3/4 x 11 3/4") tubes
(even more if the diameter is less)

White tissue or kraft paper

Foam: two squares, 26 x 26 cm
(10 1/4 x 10 1/4") (3 cm [1 1/8"] thick)

Faux fur, 35 x 35 cm (13 3/4 x 13 3/4"),
orange or lime green

Acrylic satin paint: raspberry or lime green

Wallpaper paste

Paintbrush

Tools

Cutting mat

Utility knife and blades (18 mm [3/4"])

Hot glue gun and glue sticks

Ruler

Tape measure

Cutting rule

Compass

Try square

Jigsaw or handsaw

Roll of kraft tape

Drawing pencil and black marker

Building the Stool

1 On double-wall cardboard (or triple-corrugated if you have any), draw and cut out two disks, each with a diameter of 26 cm (10 1/4"). Depending on the size of your tubes, cut them into lengths of 30 cm (11 3/4") with the jigsaw or the hand saw.

2 Use one of the cardboard disks as a template to draw and cut out the same shape from the foam material.

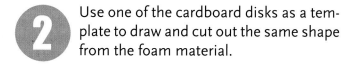

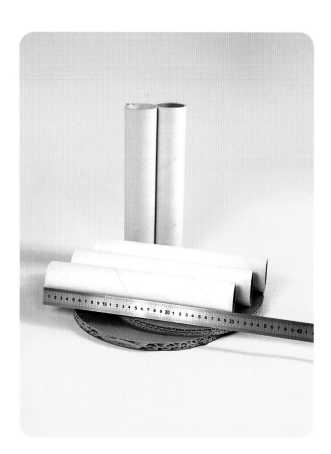

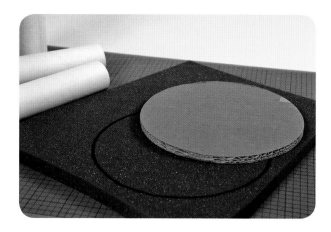

3 Cut out the disks from the foam material with scissors.

4 Hot-glue the cardboard tubes around the inner edge of one of the cardboard disks, positioning them right to the edge of the disk. Glue the tubes side by side, making sure you leave no space between them. Once you have done the outside, glue more tubes in the middle to fill the remaining space.

5 Glue the other cardboard disk to the top of the tubes.

6 On double-wall cardboard, draw and cut a strip that is the same height as the stool and has a length that is slightly longer (by about 3 cm [1 1/8]) than the total perimeter. Mold the cardboard to bend it (see "Introduction," p. 15 or p. 29). Put this to one side for now—you will glue it later.

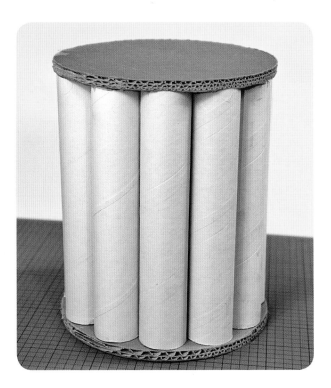

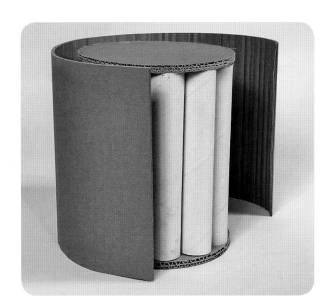

Glue the foam circle to the top of the stool with a simple bead of hot glue placed in the center of the circle.

 Lay the faux fur over the top and center it on the stool. Cut the fur around the perimeter, leaving a 5 cm (2") allowance around the outside.

 With the hot glue gun, dot some beads of glue around the top of the tubes in order to keep the faux fur in place.

10 Take the strip of cardboard that we cut in step 6 and gradually glue it around the perimeter of the stool, at the top and bottom, tucking the fur into the cardboard.

11 Tear pieces of white tissue paper. Tearing the tissue paper is better than cutting it with scissors, as the cut lines do not appear under the paint. Apply it with wallpaper paste all over the stool, overlapping the edges slightly so as to not leave any cardboard visible. Let it dry so that the water in the paste fully evaporates from the cardboard. This process is necessary prep for the paint.

Finishing Touches

Paint the stools in raspberry or lime green.
Let them dry before applying a second coat.

Bubble Bureau

Totally rounded, this unit would be ideal in a living room, where rectangular volumes are most common. Equipped with both drawers and shelves, its storage capacity is balanced wonderfully with its penchant for displaying objects. The front of the unit is set back, giving the piece a unique touch.

Materials and Finishing

Cardboard: 7 double-wall sheets, 1.42 x 1.15 m (4 5/8 x 3 3/4')

Additional double-wall cardboard for crosspieces, drawer and case linings, and exterior covering

A roll of textured lime green paper (55 cm [21 5/8"] wide): 10 m (33')

A roll of textured chocolate-colored paper (55 cm [21 5/8"] wide): 3 m (10')

Chocolate acrylic paint (matte or satin)

Tissue or kraft paper

Wallpaper paste

8 wooden curtain rings (4 cm [1 1/2"] diameter)

Colorless, water-based parquet sealant

Paintbrushes

Tools

Cutting mat

Utility knife and blades (18 mm [3/4"])

Hot glue gun and glue sticks

Ruler

Tape measure

Cutting rule

Try square

Jigsaw

Compass

Sandpaper (coarse and fine grades)

Sanding block

Roll of kraft tape (3.5 cm [1 3/8"] wide)

Drawing pencil and black marker

Building the Bureau

1 Trim the base of each of the seven sheets of cardboard with the utility knife to leave a clean, flat edge, aligning corrugations vertically with the help of the try square. Lay the seven sheets on top of each other by lining up their cut bases, and fasten them together with kraft tape so they do not slip during cutting.

2 With a pencil, draw the two inside and outside curves of the unit on the top sheet, as shown in Figure A. The center of the outside circle is situated 43 cm (17") from the bottom of the sheets and that of the inner circle is situated at 49 cm (19 3/8"). Once your lines are final, go over them in black marker.

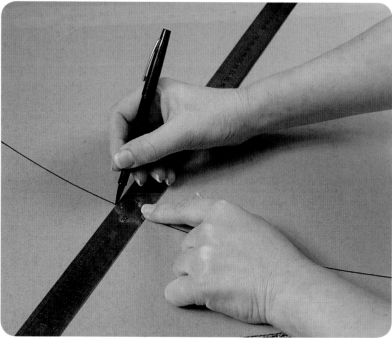

 Tip

To draw a circle of this dimension, use a 1 m ruler (yard stick) and a screw. Slide the screw into the hole of the ruler and screw it into the center of the intended circle (at either 43 cm [17"] or 49 cm [19 3/8"] from the base). Position your pencil on the desired point and rotate the ruler, keeping the pencil where it is in order to draw your circle.

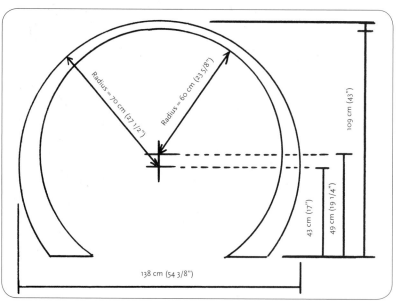

Figure A. General shape.

92

3 Cut out the exterior outline of the unit (the outer circle, so to speak) with the jigsaw, making sure you cut through all seven sheets. Stick kraft tape along the cut lines so that the sheets do not slide.

4 Separate the sheets by cutting the kraft tape away, and take two sheets for the next step. Fix these two sheets together with kraft tape, and with the jigsaw, cut along the inner circle line. Separate these two sheets and number them as sheet 1 (the front) and sheet 7 (the back).

5 To strengthen the front of the unit, hot-glue sheets 1 and 2 together.

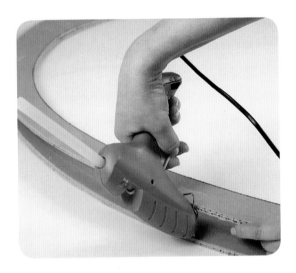

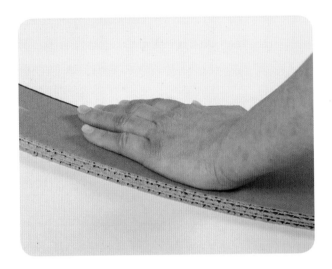

6 Put sheet 7 (the back sheet) to one side and attach sheets 3, 4, 5, and 6 together by sticking kraft tape along the perimeter so that they do not slide. Be sure to align their bases. With a pencil, draw the locations of the shelf and the drawers on the top sheet according to Figure B. Once your lines are final, go over them in black marker. Cut out the cases and drawers with the jigsaw, making sure you cut through all four sheets. Reapply kraft tape to the cut edges so the sheets do not slide. Put aside the fronts of the drawers. Sand down all of the cut edges with fine sandpaper.

The seven cut sheets at this stage.

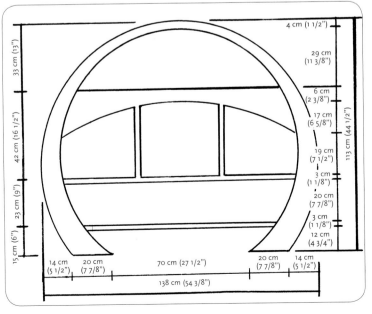

Figure B.

93

7 Reattach sheets 3, 4, 5, and 6 together with kraft tape. On the top sheet (sheet 3), draw all of the slots around the arc of the unit, with each one 0.7 cm (9/23") wide, as shown on Figure C. Cut them with the utility knife up to the midpoint (the solid black lines). Each slot has a different height depending on its position.

Figure C. The slots around the circle.

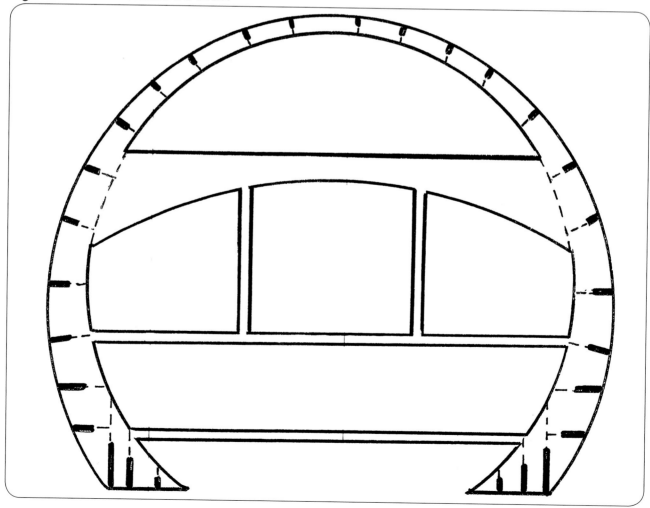

8 Separate the four sheets by cutting the kraft tape away and put sheet 3 (the top sheet) to one side. Now attach sheets 4, 5, and 6 with kraft tape so that they do not slide. On the central part of the sheets, draw and cut the inner slots with the utility knife, following Figure D.

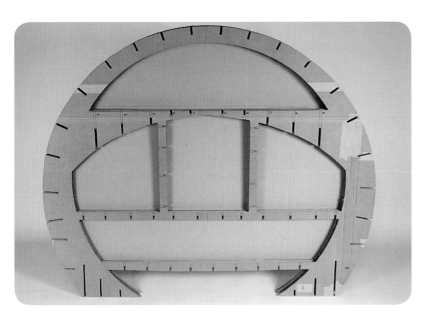

Figure D. The inside slots.

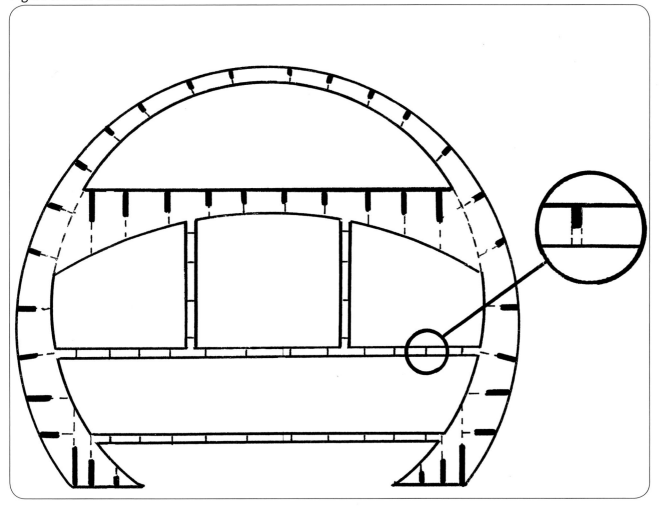

9 Take sheet 4 and put it against sheet 7 (the back sheet). Pencil on sheet 7 all the locations of the cut slots. Then, still using sheet 4 as a guide, pencil the positions of these slots on the back of sheets 1 and 2, which are glued together (the front of the unit), as well as on the back of sheet 3.

10 Using double-wall cardboard, draw and cut out the crosspieces according to Figure E. Those that will fit close up to the arc (the outside ones) are 32 cm (12 1/2") long, and those that will be on the inner side of the structure will be 28.3 cm (11 1/8") long. Their height will vary depending on where they are positioned. On the longer sections, draw and cut four slots that are half the height of the cross section and 0.7 cm (1/4") wide. On the shorter sections, draw and cut three slots following the same principle. When cutting them, number each cross section as well as its position to help make assembling the structure easier.

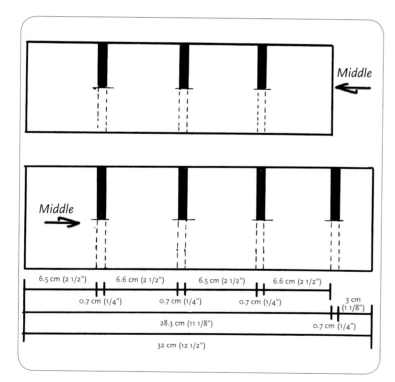

Figure E. The crosspieces.

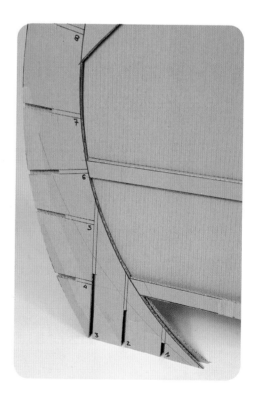

The numbering of the slots that will accommodate the crosspieces.

11 Fit all the crosspieces into the corresponding slots, starting with those on the outside first. Those that are longer will help to stabilize the structure.

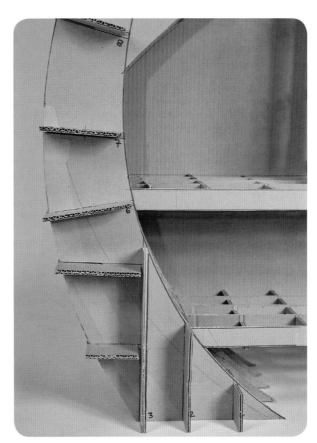

12 Once the crosspieces have been fitted, secure them to sheet 7 (the back sheet) with the glue gun, then to sheet 3 (front of the shelving), and finally the facade (sheets 1 and 2 glued together), following the outlines of the slots.

13 Line the inner cases with sheets of double-wall cardboard. For this, measure their width and depth, from the back up to the covering of the front sheet. The visible corrugations on the surface of the cardboard must be placed towards the front and the back. Start by covering the top and the bottom of the cases. For the top, which is a rounded shape, measure the height with a flexible tape measure, anticipating a little extra length (say 1 to 2 mm [1/32 to 1/16"]). Cut the sheets with a utility knife and mold them over the edge of a table or with the help of a tube in order to give them more of a curved shape, to follow that of the cases. Try them before the final gluing process, and then glue them with a thin line of glue on the back cut edge. Once dry, glue the front using a thin line of glue on the back side of the front facing.

Still using double-wall cardboard, cut out the sheets for the inner sides of the cases. Do not cover the inner part of the cases that corresponds to the bigger arc (outer circle)—you will do this in the following stage.

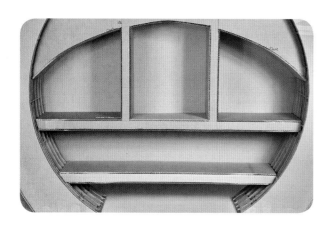

14 Once the insides of the cases have been glued, you are going to cover the inside of the bigger arc (outer circle). You will have to make some joints in the sheets, because this is a big surface (see "Joining Cardboard Sheets," p. 8). For the width of the strips, measure the depth of the unit from the back up to the front facing. Mold the sheets over the edge of a table or with the help of a tube to give them a curved shape that will follow the curvature of the unit. To allow for the shelving, draw it in pencil first. Test each sheet several times before gluing.

15 Once your sheets are ready, hot-glue them, working in small sections, starting with the back edge and finishing up with the inside of the facing. Do this all around the inner surface of the arc.

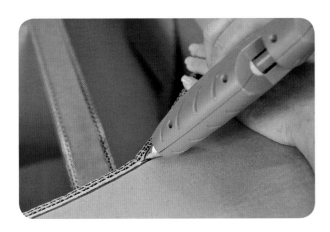

16 To cover the outside of the unit, draw and cut long sheets of double-wall cardboard so the length is the same as the depth of the unit. Mold your sheets, placing the corrugations facing front so the cardboard bends more easily. You will have to combine some pieces—make sure you square up the bottom of each sheet. Hot-glue them to the inside edges of the cut sheets, progressing in sections as the glue will set very quickly. Start under the feet and continue up the side in order to cover the entire piece.

17 Sand down the whole unit (edges, front, and back) starting with the coarse sandpaper and finishing with the fine. Remove the dust from the sanding process, then apply kraft tape along all the visible corrugations and edges as well as the inside edges of the cases. For curves, apply kraft tape along the edges and notch with scissors before folding and sticking down.

The Drawers

1 For the drawer facing, use the cut-outs from step 6 as a guide. Take off 0.7 cm (1/4”) in width around the curved side of the drawers: on the outside for the smaller drawers, and on the two sides of the bigger drawer. Then, reinforce each template by gluing on double-wall cardboard of the same dimensions. Cut out the facing pieces with the utility knife. Sand down and dust. Apply kraft tape around the outside, folding it over the sides and notching with scissors at the curves.

2 For the interior and the assembly of the drawers, follow steps 3-5 from the "Introduction" on page 17-18. Then, repeat steps 6 and 7 from the introduction like this: at the back of the facing of the two side drawers and the big drawer below them, draw the lines 0.7 cm (1/4”) from the edge, following the dotted lines from Figure F. Glue them to the facing along these lines. For the curved edges, glue along the actual cut edge of the facade. Proceed by following steps 8 and 9 from the "Introduction."

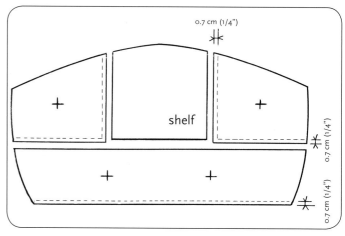

Figure F. The front of the three drawers.

3 Locate the center of the facing for each of the two smaller drawers. From the center, draw a circle 4 cm (1 1/2") in diameter. Do the same for the larger drawer, but instead draw two circles (see Figure F). Cut these circles out with the jigsaw. Their diameter will match that of the wooden rings that will be inserted.

Finishing Touches

Painting the Unit

1 Prepare the surfaces to be painted in the chocolate color: the back of the large case at the top (not that of the middle or the drawers), the facing around the cases and the drawers, and the underside of the large drawer. Tear pieces of tissue or kraft paper—tearing is better than cutting with scissors because cut edges could show under the paint. Apply it with wallpaper paste, covering the entire unit. Overlap the tissue paper slightly so no cardboard is left visible. There is no need to do the front of the drawers as these will be covered with paper. Leave to dry so that the water in the paste fully evaporates from the cardboard.

2 Paint the back of the top case, the front facing around the cases, and the drawers with the chocolate-colored paint. Paint slightly over the inside edges of the cases and the drawers so there is some color behind the covering paper. Apply two or even three coats, depending on the quality of your paint, letting everything dry between coats.

3 Also, paint the eight wooden rings in chocolate after lightly sanding them.

Fitting the Paper

1 With the wallpaper paste, start by gluing the lime green paper to the front of the outside circle, leaving a 0.5 cm (1/4") allowance above and below that you will fold and glue down. If your paper has lines, be sure to position them correctly, particularly when making seams. To keep your transition areas neat, overlap the two sheets of paper and cut through both at the same time. Get rid of the left over paper: the two edges will meet perfectly.

2 With the same lime green paper, cut strips for the inside depth of the unit, adding a 1.5 cm (5/8") allowance you can fold at the back. The stripes on the paper should lie horizontally when you look at the unit from the side. Glue them flush with the edge at the front (they will cover the excess 0.5 cm [1/4"] that is folded at the front already), and fold the 1.5 cm (5/8") at the back after notching with scissors.

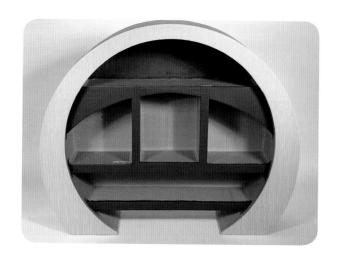

3 Placing the stripes vertically, cut and glue a strip of lime green paper to cover the back of the middle case, adding an allowance of 0.5 cm (1/4") around the outside. Then, cover the inside of the case with strips of lime green paper that are exactly the width of the inside. Also, cut some chocolate-colored paper to cover the sides and the top of the top case.

4 To cover the fronts of the drawers with chocolate paper, lay each of them on the back of the paper and draw the outline with an excess of 0.5 cm (1/4") around the perimeter. Cut and glue down the allowance by folding the edges and notching with scissors on the curves. For the holes, cut the paper in lines radiating from a center point. Then glue a 2 cm (3/4") wide strip of chocolate paper all around the front of the drawer, positioning it at the edge of the front facing and folding the paper at the back, after having notched it with scissors.

5 Hot-glue the wooden rings in the holes. Two rings are needed for each hole, given that the cardboard used for the front of the drawers has been doubled. In each hole, push in the first ring and glue, making sure you push it through the thickness of the front facing to the back; push the second one through and glue it so it sits flush with the front facing.

6 To finish, varnish the whole unit (including the inside) with two coats. Let it dry between coats. It is advisable to do a test run with the varnish on a bit of scrap paper first—on some darker papers, varnish has a tendency to darken (or lighten) colors, or leave streaks if the coats are too thick.

Mansard Headboard

In this loft conversion, a headboard, flanked by two bedside tables, is adapted for the sloping roof. If you don't have the space available for the whole design, you can choose to make just the headboard or just the two bedside tables. Likewise, the dimensions must be adapted depending on how much space is available and the size of your bed (140 cm [55"] in this design), while using the same design principles.

Materials and Finishing

Cardboard: 3 double-wall sheets, 2.90 x 1.02m (9 1/2 x 3 3/8')*

Additional double-wall cardboard for crosspieces, the lining of cases and drawers, and exterior covering

10 sheets of chocolate-colored Nepalese paper (approximately 50 x 70 cm [19 3/4 x 27 1/2"])

7 sheets of patterned, orange-colored Nepalese paper (approximately 50 x 70 cm [19 3/4 x 27 1/2"])

Wallpaper paste

Colorless, water-based parquet sealant

Paintbrushes

2 matching drawer pulls with screws, washers, and 2 nuts

Tools

Cutting mat

Utility knife and blades (18 mm [3/4"])

Hot glue gun and glue sticks

Ruler

Tape measure

Cutting rule

Try square

Jigsaw

Sandpaper (coarse and fine grades)

Sanding block

Roll of kraft tape (3.5 cm [1 3/8"] wide)

Drawing pencil and black marker

Screwdriver

Drill and drill bit the same diameter as the drawer pull screws

*It may be difficult to obtain sheets of cardboard this length. In this case, combine sheets (see "Introduction," p. 8).

Building the Headboard Unit

1 Trim the base of each of the three sheets of cardboard with the utility knife to leave a clean, flat edge, aligning corrugations vertically with the help of the try square. Number the sheets from 1 to 3 (1 being the front sheet and 3 the back). Lay them on top of each other, aligning their cut bases. Fasten them together with kraft tape along the whole perimeter so they do not slip during the cutting process.

2 With a pencil, draw the general design of the unit on sheet 1, following Figure A. Once your lines are final, go over them in black marker.

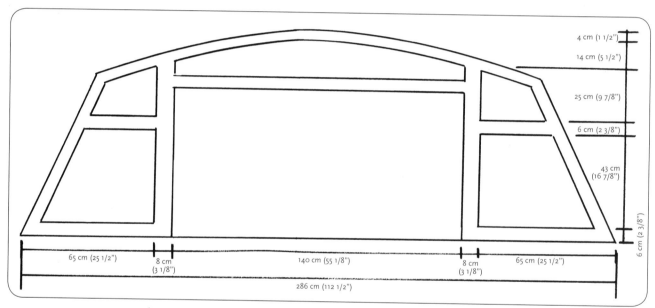

Figure A. Shape and dimensions.

3 Cut out the exterior outline of the unit with the jigsaw (or the utility knife, given that there are only three sheets in this design), making sure you cut through all three. Apply kraft tape as you cut so that the sheets do not slide. Lightly sand down all the edges.

4 Separate the sheets by cutting away the kraft tape with a knife and put sheet 3 (the back sheet) to one side. Fasten the other two sheets (1 and 2) together with kraft tape; with the jigsaw (or the utility knife) cut out the cases, the inside of the two drawers, and the central rectangle which will accommodate the bed. Set aside this large rectangle and the cut-outs from the drawers, as these will be used as guides.

5 Separate sheets 1 and 2 again. On sheet 2, draw all of the 0.7 cm (1/4") slots, as shown on Figure B, and cut them out with the knife, going to the midpoint (as shown with the solid black lines). Each slot has a different height depending on its position.

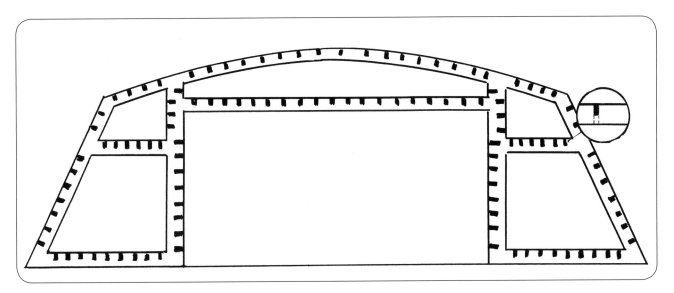

Figure B. The slots.

6 Put sheet 2 against sheet 3 (the back sheet). With the pencil, mark on sheet 3 all of the positions of the slots. Then, with the help of sheet 2, draw the positions of these slots on to the back of sheet 1 (the front sheet).

7 On double-wall cardboard, draw and cut out the crosspieces. All of them are 24.7 cm (9 3/4") in length, and their height will vary depending on their positioning. On each of them, draw and cut out a slot whose height will be half that of the cross section and 0.7 cm (1/4") wide. During the cutting process, number each cross section as well as its position on the central sheet so you can locate them more easily during the assembly of the structure.

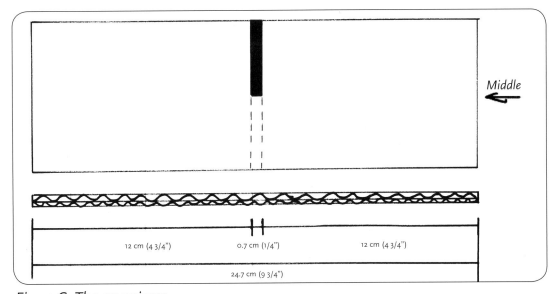

Figure C. The crosspieces.

8 Fit all of the crosspieces into central sheet 2.

9 Once the crosspieces have been fitted, hot-glue them to sheet 3 (the back) and then to the front (sheet 1) where you have drawn on their respective positions.

10 Draw and cut long strips of cardboard 20 cm (7 7/8") tall, positioning the corrugations in a way that allows you to bend the width of the strips. Bend them into zig-zag shapes and glue them into the large rectangular opening, following Figure D.

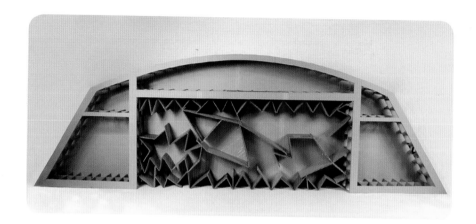

Figure D.

11 Re-use the large rectangle that was cut out in step 4 and glue it to the zigzag cardboard, fitting it between the bedside tables.

12 From double-wall cardboard, cut sheets to cover the inside of the cases. For this, measure the width and the length, from the back to the front facing. Place the visible corrugations towards you, facing front. Start with the top and the bottom of the cases. Apply a thin line of hot glue to the back cut edge; when it is dry, glue the front with a thin line of glue on the inside of the front facing. Proceed in the same way for the side sheets on the inside of the cases.

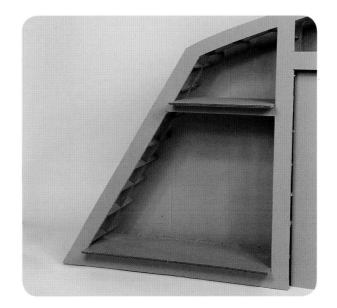

13 To cover the outside of the unit, draw and cut sheets of double-wall cardboard with a length equal to that of the depth of the unit. Glue them to the outside of the unit (including the underside), placing the corrugations towards the front so that the cardboard bends more easily. Make the necessary joints following the instructions on p. 15.

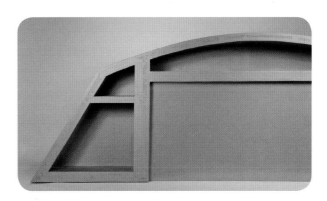

14 Sand down all of the corrugations on the unit (edges, front, and back) starting with the coarse sandpaper and finishing with the fine. Then apply strips of kraft tape along all the visible corrugations and edges of the cases. For curves, apply kraft tape along the corrugations and notch with scissors before folding and sticking down.

15 Use the two cut-outs from step 4 that correspond to the fronts of the drawers, and back them with another sheet of cardboard of the same size (with the corrugations positioned vertically) and hot-glue them together. Sand the surfaces and apply kraft tape along the perimeter. For this, stick the strip over the edge and fold it over each side.
For the inside and assembly of the drawers, follow steps 3-5 of the introduction on pages 17-18. Replace steps 6 and 7 from the introduction as follows: on the back of each facing piece, draw a line 0.7 cm (9/23") from the bottom, and a right angled line along each side, 0.7 cm (9/23") from the edge. Glue your drawer block to the front and continue by following steps 8 and 9 from the "Introduction."

Finishing Touches

1 With the wallpaper paste, apply patterned orange paper to the front of the two drawers, leaving an allowance of 0.5 cm (1/4") around the outside. Then, fold and stick down the excess. For a neater finish, cut a 2 cm (3/4") wide strip with the same paper. Paste it to the edge of the front along the whole perimeter of the surface, and fold the excess to the back.

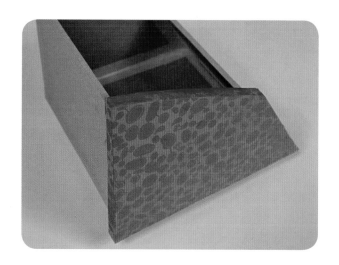

2 Apply the same paper to the back of the cases in the bedside tables and at the back of the large central case, too. Seams will need to be made in the paper to cover the back of the large case. To keep your transitions neat, align the edges of the paper and cut both sheets at the same time. Get rid of the excess paper: the two edges should meet perfectly.

3 With the wallpaper paste, start by sticking the chocolate Nepalese paper to the front of the unit. Paste pieces of the paper to overlap slightly so the cardboard underneath doesn't show, and to achieve an embossed, textured effect. Overrun the inside of the cases slightly to make up for the thinness of the material. Leave to dry.

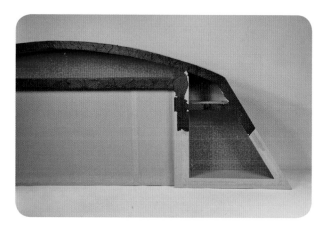

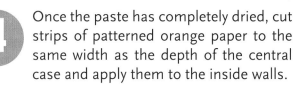 Once the paste has completely dried, cut strips of patterned orange paper to the same width as the depth of the central case and apply them to the inside walls.

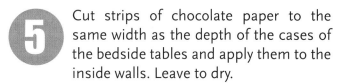 Cut strips of chocolate paper to the same width as the depth of the cases of the bedside tables and apply them to the inside walls. Leave to dry.

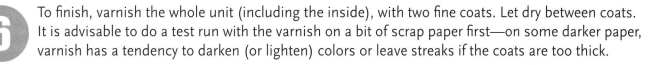 To finish, varnish the whole unit (including the inside), with two fine coats. Let dry between coats. It is advisable to do a test run with the varnish on a bit of scrap paper first—on some darker paper, varnish has a tendency to darken (or lighten) colors or leave streaks if the coats are too thick.

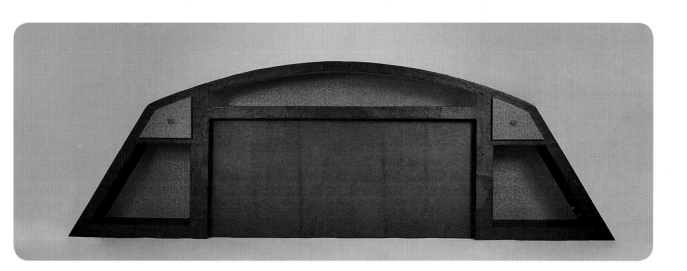

Mark the center of the front of the drawers, and drill a hole with the same diameter as the drawer pull screw. Under the head of each screw, on the inside of the drawer, place a metal washer so as not to tear the cardboard, and then screw tight with a nut.

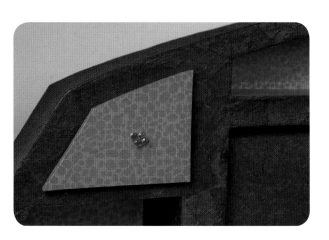

Serpentine Column

This serpentine column will fit into the room of your choice, bringing with it a decisively original touch. Five different sized drawers give it an advantage for storing a number of things, thus combining decorative design and practicality. But you may well decide to have shelves instead of drawers...

Your choice of finishing touches (paper, paint, and drawer pulls) will determine the style of this unit.

Materials and Finishings

Cardboard: 4 double-wall sheets, 1.40 x 0.57 m (4 5/8 x 1 7/8')

Additional double-wall cardboard for crosspieces, case and drawer linings, and exterior covering

Acrylic satin paint: Light grey

Roll of colored paper (55 cm [22"] wide): 4.5 m (14 3/4")

White tissue or kraft paper

Wallpaper paste

5 brushed-aluminium drawer pulls, with screws

5 metal washers

Colorless, water-based sealant

Paintbrushes

Tools

Cutting mat

Utility knife and blades (18 mm [3/4"])

Hot glue gun and glue sticks

Ruler

Tape measure

Cutting rule

Try square

Jigsaw

Sandpaper (different grades)

Sanding block

Roll of kraft tape

Drawing pencil and black marker

Drill and drill bit the same diameter as the drawer pull screws

Screwdriver

Building the Column

1 Trim the base of each of the four sheets to leave a clean, flat edge, aligning corrugations vertically with the help of the try square. Then lay the four sheets on top of each other, aligning their cut bases. Fasten them together by applying kraft tape along the edges so that they do not slide during cutting.

2 Following Figure A, draw the general outline of the column, as well as the outlines for the cases, on the top sheet. Once your lines are final, go over them in black marker.

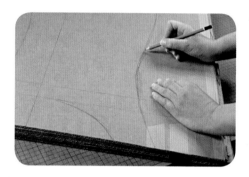

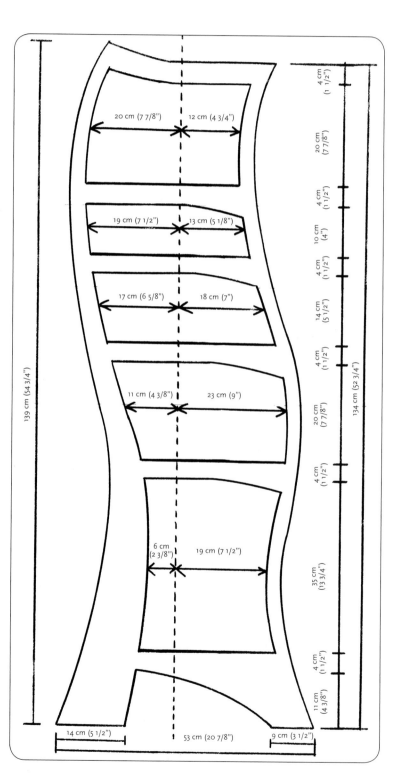

Figure A. General shape and dimensions.

3 With the jigsaw, cut out the outline of the column, making sure you cut through all four sheets. Do not cut the cases of the drawers just yet. Apply kraft tape as you cut so that the sheets do not slip. Sand down all of the cut edges with medium sand paper.

4 Separate the four sheets by cutting the kraft tape away with a knife. Put the back sheet to one side (to use later for the back of the unit) and number it as sheet 4. Then number the other three 1 to 3 starting with the top sheet (the front), maintaining the order from the cutting process. With the kraft tape, fix sheets 1, 2, and 3 together again in order to cut the inside of the drawers with the jigsaw. Put these cut-outs to one side—you will need to use them as guides when making the drawers. Lightly sand down all of the sheets to get rid of any excess material left by the jigsaw.

5 Separate the sheets again and put sheet 1 (the front sheet) to one side. With kraft tape, fix sheets 2 and 3 together in order to draw on the 0.7 cm (1/4") slots, as shown in Figure B. Cut them with the utility knife, going to the midpoint (as shown with the solid black lines). Each slot will have a different height depending on its position.

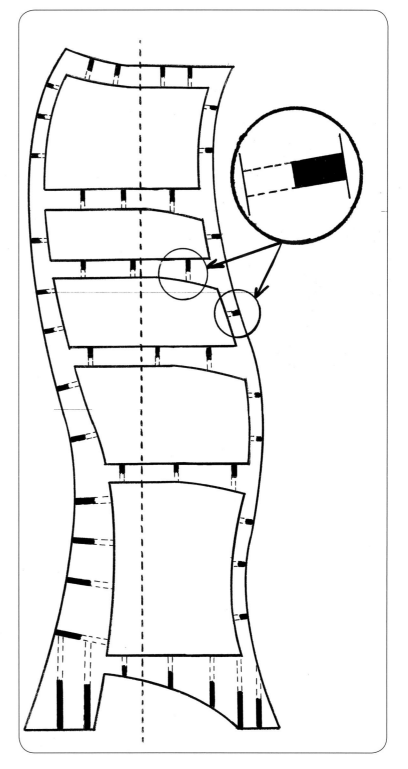

Figure B. The cut-out drawers and slots.

6 On double-wall cardboard, draw and cut out the crosspieces. They will all be 28 cm (11") long and their height will vary depending on their position. On each of them, cut two slots that go to the midpoint of the cardboard and are 0.7 cm (1/4") wide. When cutting them, number each cross section and mark their position on the central sheets (sheets 2 and 3), making the assembly of the structure easier.

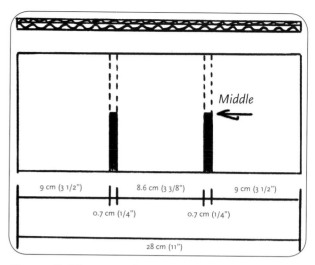

Figure C. The crosspieces.

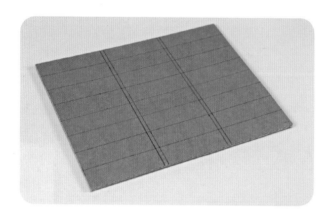 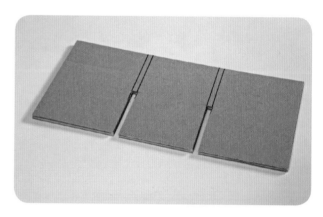

7 Then put sheet 2, the sheet with all the cut slots, on sheet 4 (the back sheet) to mark the positions in pencil. Use sheet 2 again to mark the positions of the slots on the back of sheet 1. This gives you reference points when gluing the structure to the front and back sheets.

8 Fit the crosspieces on to sheets 2 and 3, using your numbering system.

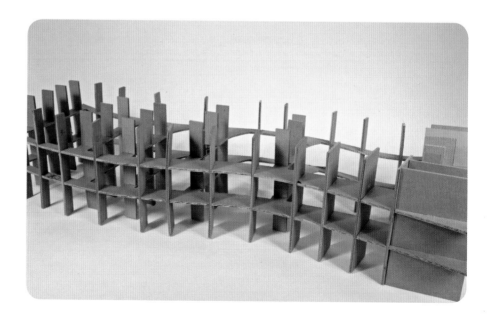

9 Once the crosspieces have been fitted into the center sheets, lay sheet 4 (the back sheet) flat on your work table and position the central structure, following the slot markings. Glue the surface of each cross section on to sheet 4 using the hot glue gun, then proceed in the same way, gluing the structure to the front facing (sheet 1). Be careful not to leave any glue on the inside or outside surfaces of the unit because this will hamper covering the unit.

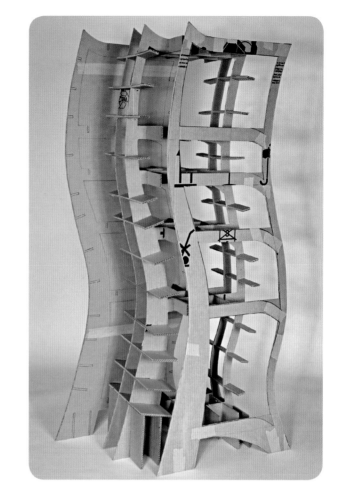

10 With the structure now glued to the back and the front, line the interior of the cases, at the top and the bottom, using double-wall cardboard. For this, measure the width and the depth, from the back to the covering of the front sheet. The visible corrugations on the surface must be placed towards the front and the back. The sheets at the top must follow the curvature of the cases—measure the width with a tape measure. Allow a little more (say, 1 to 2 mm [1/32 to 1/16"] extra) and mold the sheets over the edge of a table or with the help of a tube to give them a curved shape (see p. 15 or p. 29). Cut the sheets with the utility knife and test them before the final gluing. Start by gluing the back cut edge to the back facing; once dry, glue the front by putting a thin line of glue on the inside of the front facing.

11 On double-wall cardboard, now cut sheets to cover the sides of the cases. For those that are curved, measure their height with a tape measure. Allow a little more in the height (say, 1 to 2 mm [1/32 to 1/16"]) and mold the sheets over the edge of a table or with a tube to give them a curved shape, which will follow the design of the unit. Test them before the final gluing process.

12 To cover the outside of the column, cut strips of double-wall cardboard to the same width as the depth of the unit, laying the corrugations horizontally and facing front so that the cardboard bends more easily. For the length to cover the the whole exterior of the unit, you will have to join several sheets together (see "Joining Sheets of Cardboard," p. 8). Make sure you square off each sheet with the try square. In order to bend the cardboard so that it follows the curves, mold it over the edge of a table or with a tube, changing the curve to follow the design. Put the column on its back, using your work table as a guide so that your sheets are squared off, hot-gluing them in sections, as the glue will set very quickly. Start underneath the feet. Continue up the sides and finish on top.

13 Still using the double-wall cardboard, draw and cut out the bottom of the drawers, making them 1 cm (3/8") less deep than the cases. As for the width, the drawers must be able to slide without sticking. Then, draw and cut the two lateral sides of each drawer, following the shape of the column, with the corrugations horizontal if the side is curved. Their depth is equal to the bottom of the drawer and their height must be 1 cm (3/8") less than that of the case, to avoid sticking.

14 Sand down the whole unit. For the visible corrugations and the ridges, position your sanding block flat so as not to damage the edges. Remove dust from the sanding process, and then apply strips of kraft tape along all the visible corrugations and the edges. For curves, apply kraft tape along the corrugations, notching with scissors. Then fold it over and glue down.

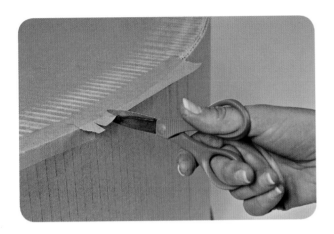

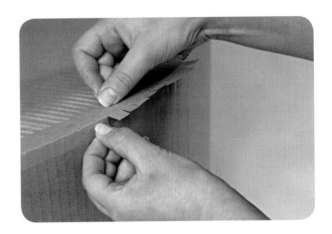

15 For the drawers, start by making the fronts according to Figure D. Draw them on two double-wall sheets of cardboard that have been glued together. You can use the templates cut in step 4 by adding the acute line at the lower right corner of each facing (outline that dips below the dotted lines in the figure). Cut each drawer facing out with the utility knife and apply kraft tape around the outside. For this, place the strip over the edge and fold it over each side, notching with scissors for any curves.

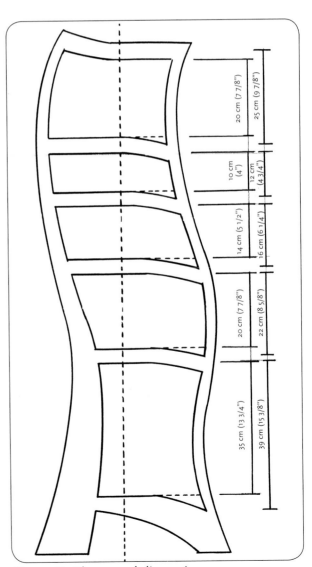

Figure D. Shape and dimensions.

16 Continue making the drawers following steps 3-9 from the introduction, pages 17-20.

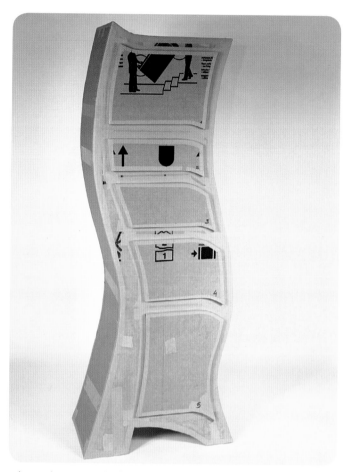

The column with five drawers in place, before finishing.

Finishing Touches

Painting the Unit and Fitting the Paper

1 Tear out pieces of white tissue paper. Tearing is better than cutting with scissors because cut edges could show under the paint. Apply the pieces to the front and back of the column (the areas that will be painted) with wallpaper paste, remembering to overlap the edges slightly so no cardboard is left visible. Let it dry so that all of the water in the paste evaporates from the cardboard. This process is necessary for prepping the surface for painting.

2 With the satin paint, paint the front and the back of the column, painting over the edges of the sides and the inside of the cases, as these will be covered with paper. Also paint the surface of the front of the drawers. Apply two coats; let it dry between each. Once the paint is dry, apply kraft tape to the inside perimeter of the cases of the drawers to achieve a neater finish.

3 Measure and cut two strips of decorative paper to the same width as the depth of the column, removing 1 or 2 mm (1/32 to 1/16") from the sides so that the paper does not fray at the edges. For the height, add a 2 cm (3/4") allowance on top and 5 cm (2") below. With the wallpaper paste, stick a strip to each side of the unit, folding the excess over. Then apply a strip of paper (with no allowance) to cover the top of the unit.

To cover the front of the drawers, put each front on to the back of the paper and trace the outline. Cut and glue this paper to the drawer fronts.

Wait for the glue to dry completely, and then varnish the whole column, applying two thin coats and letting it dry between each.

The Drawer Pulls

1 Mark the center point of each drawer front and pierce a hole the same diameter as the screws using the drill or a borer. On the head of each screw, on the inside of the drawer, position a flat metal washer in order to avoid tearing the cardboard, and then screw on the pulls.

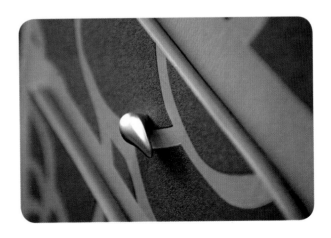

GALLERY

The Valentine Wardrobe

For this softly curved wardrobe, I prefer to use untreated cardboard, leaving the original print visible. On the front of the drawers, Nepalese paper brings color to the design, as do the strip accents along the inside of the unit. The natural wood drawer pulls complement the color of the cardboard. The whole wardrobe is varnished.

The Seventies Lamp

This eccentric lamp, influenced by the 70s, is made with untreated cardboard and a cardboard tube (apart from the shade itself). The sides are covered in Nepalese paper.

The Cube Lamp

This lamp is made with untreated cardboard, including the rings.

Reception Area

For a company that puts scrap to use-metal, wood, paper, cardboard-I designed and built a reception area that consists of a three-seat sofa, two armchairs, two stools, a coffee table, a magazine rack, and a lamp.
We chose red and cardboard-brown Nepalese paper with a special application for an embossed effect.

Aurore Column

The five drawers in this tower have flat or curved bases following the curves of the design. To match the olive green satin paint, the front of the drawers are covered with old style green marbled paper and fitted with brass pulls.

Louna Armchair

This ergonomic, contemporary armchair is covered with varnished orange Skivertex paper, which harmonizes with the chocolate-colored cushions.

Jeanne's Elephant

This elephant is integrated into a little girl's bedroom that has jungle décor. With ten drawers and four shelves…even the trunk can be used to store socks! The whole unit is covered in Nepalese paper with discreet translucent pulls, plus a black one for the eye.

Lison Bedside Tables

These two rounded bedside tables are designed for a little girl's room. Each table has a drawer and a shelf covered with plum and lime green Nepalese paper. The "wave" pulls are matte gold.

Children's Toutankarton Armchair

Made for a room shared by two children, this pharaonic armchair is covered in gold and red tissue paper. The golden decorative balls trimmed with red tassels perfect the finish of this chair. The whole creation is varnished. (Toutankarton is a pun on Tutankhamun and the French *tout en carton*—"everything in cardboard"!)

Emma and Martin's Elephant

This children's bookcase can furnish a landing shared by two bedrooms. The specs: it's an animal, it's not too deep, and it doesn't hide the power outlet or a switch. A drawer is built into the head and another one is between the front two feet. The lower shelves hold Emma's large books and her big brother's comics are held at the top, in the ear.... The elephant is finished with paint and African-themed Décopatch paper. A black drawer pull is used to create the eye.

KIKI CARTON

A former event and trade show planner with experience creating displays, Kiki Carton has been "cardboarding" for 6 years, pushing the limits of this reusable material. She lives in France where she teaches cardboard workshops and creates furniture on commission.